THE
WHOLE FAMILY
COOKBOOK

THE
WHOLE FAMILY
COOKBOOK

TWO-TIERED MEALS TO PLEASE
BOTH PARENTS AND KIDS

KRISTENE FORTIER

ILLUSTRATIONS BY CHRIS PARK

A BIRCH LANE PRESS BOOK
Published by Carol Publishing Group

To my family:
Brad,
Casey, and Michelle

Copyright © 1998 Kristene Fortier

A Birch Lane Press Book
Published by Carol Publishing Group
Birch Lane Press is a registered trademark of Carol Communications, Inc.

Editorial, sales and distribution, rights and permissions inquiries should be addressed to Carol Publishing Group, 120 Enterprise Avenue, Secaucus, N.J. 07094.

In Canada: Canadian Manda Group, One Atlantic Avenue, Suite 105, Toronto, Ontario M6K 3E7.

Carol Publishing books may be purchased in bulk at special discounts for sales promotion, fund-raising, or educational purposes. Special editions can be created to specifications. For details, contact Special Sales Department, 120 Enterprise Avenue, Secaucus, N.J. 07094.

Manufactured in the United States of America
10 9 8 7 6 5 4 3 2 1

Library of Congress Cataloging-in-Publication Data

Fortier, Kristene.
The whole family cookbook : two-tiered meals to please both parents and kids / Kristene Fortier.
p.   cm.
"A Birch Lane Press book."
Includes index.
ISBN 1-55972-481-1 (hc.)
1. Cookery.   I. Title.
TX714.F68   1998
641.5—dc21   98–27269
CIP

Contents

ACKNOWLEDGMENTS

A special thanks to Brad, my husband of twenty-two years, for his support and encouragement and to my children, Casey and Michelle. They were the catalyst that started this whole process. Thanks to Rita and Avis for their guidance. Thanks to all of my testers and their families, including: Cathy Vonder Porton, Jytte Langlois, Judy Garber, Margaret Butler-Terry, Vivian Clausing, Catriona Kennedy, Ann Rojas, Sylvia Wuensche-Wienands, Ann Shields, Nancy Cottong, Inger Birchofberger, Jeanne Fitzsimmons, Mimi Conley, Kathleen Lawson, and Chris Park.

INTRODUCTION

Several years ago, I was a full time, high-tech manager in Silicon Valley. I began my day before 6 A.M. With an hour to get ready and drop off my infant son at day care, I had just enough time to make my forty-five-minute commute to my job at Apple Computer. There I worked at a frenetic pace all day so that I could rush out of the office at precisely 5 P.M. to pick up my son before the center closed. Even though my husband and I switched off regularly, when our son was sick we frantically compared our busy schedules to decide who would stay home to care for him.

I tried job sharing. While I worked fewer hours, I still didn't have the flexibility that I needed. When my second child was born, I made the decision to stay at home. I wanted to be with my children when school let out. I wanted to be there when they did their homework. I wanted to teach them my sense of values and ethics. I wanted their lives to be enriched with sports, music, or whatever activities they chose to try.

It was a difficult adjustment, both financially and emotionally. For the first time, it was awkward to be asked What do you do? While I loved being a full-time mom, I still needed a creative outlet. I read all the books about starting your own business and following your passion and dreams.

I always loved food. As a child growing up on military bases around the world, I was exposed to a wide range of international cuisines. As an adult, business travel added to my culinary education. I had always been an avid home cook and loved both the preparation and the health aspects of food. I had never thought of turning my interest in food into a serious career, but after attending several classes at the California Culinary Academy in San Francisco, I was inspired to start my own cooking school. I called it Health-Enomics, and I taught healthy cooking to time-pressed high-tech workers over the lunch hour.

Since my cooking at home was becoming increasingly influenced by my children's eating habits, I began to develop recipes for making two variations of the same meal. I submitted some of my recipes to a variety of Bay Area newspapers and magazines, and my freelance writer's career was started. The publication of *The Whole Family Cookbook* completes my transition from high-tech Silicon Valley manager to full-time mom, cooking instructor, writer, and author. I have received far more satisfaction and fulfillment from my family and my work than I ever dreamed possible.

Notes From a Well-Seasoned Mom

Before my children were born, I always had a lovely fantasy about family dinners. We're all gathered around the dinner table; we're laughing and joking and having a wonderful time. Real life turned out to be quite different: Our dinner hours were often tense and frustrating as my husband and I tried to persuade our youngsters to eat what was on their plates.

While attending a parenting seminar, I compared notes with other parents on "getting kids to eat healthy." I was surprised and delighted by what I heard. One parent after another spoke of their frustrations trying to get their youngsters to eat. "Sally has to keep all the food separated on her plate." "David only eats foods that are brown." "Ryan is a vegetarian, although he won't eat vegetables." We all had a great laugh together and I went home with a sense of relief that my children were not that different from other kids.

Like most parents, I want my children to eat healthy. But their food preferences change often and their appetites fluctuate. So when they refused to eat the meal that I prepared, I tried to find a substitute. One evening, exhausted after preparing three different meals, I realized that I had to develop a better way.

I got out the family cookbooks and tried the recipes that were "guaranteed" to please everyone. My husband and I found the food to be lacking in any distinctive flavor, and the recipes didn't make a difference with our children.

Frustrated, I changed tactics. I decided that as long as my children were going to be particular about what they ate, my husband and I would at least enjoy our meals. We love ethnic cuisine with spicy seasonings, so I began to cook the foods that we enjoy. Our children would never eat this kind of food so I separated their portions before adding the seasonings. I found that once I got started, it opened a whole new world of food for our family.

The Whole Family Cookbook is based on a philosophy that getting a healthy meal on the table that everyone enjoys is possible. Each recipe has been developed in stages and can be seasoned very simply for children or in a more sophisticated way to please adults.

I've taken into consideration the needs of busy parents who want to get dinner on the table in a hurry. The grown-up variations are generally more spicy or include ingredients that many children may not like. All of the recipes are structured in a similar manner. The common ingredients for each recipe are listed first, followed by the unique ingredients for each variation. Preparation begins with the basic ingredients, then the recipe is separated and seasoned differently.

The nutritional analysis is calculated by dividing the main ingredients in half, then adding the adults-only or children-only ingredients. Optional ingredients are not included in the analysis nor are ingredients that do not call for any specific amount, such as salt and pepper. If more than one choice for a particular ingredient is listed in a recipe, the lower-fat alternative is used to calculate the analysis. The nutritional analysis per serving is determined by using the larger of the number of servings listed. The calculations were made using the Food Processor Nutritional Analysis Software from ESHA Research, Salem, Oregon. While I've tried to be as accurate as possible, I have not specified brand names—and nutritional content can vary considerably from product to product. Use the nutritional analyses as approximations or estimates only.

Fifteen families tested the recipes in *The Whole Family Cookbook*.

Their experience preparing the recipes and subsequent feedback has been incorporated into this book. I found that many children liked the grown-ups' variation and many adults liked the children's variation. I was pleased to learn that once the testers finished testing, many incorporated the recipes into their regular menus. Each recipe can be prepared using only one of the variations by simply doubling the ingredients for the desired variation.

Our family philosophy has always been to expose our children to everything on the table. When a new food is introduced, we ask our children to take a small serving, which we call a "no-thank-you-bite." Over time they have become more adventurous and they've developed a greater tolerance for different foods. This has been a particular blessing when dining out or visiting friends. Our children can ignore foods on their plates that they don't like without making a big fuss.

However, there is no one formula that fits all kids. Remind yourself that their tastes will change continually, and if they don't like something this week, by next week it may be their favorite food.

THE WELL-EQUIPPED KITCHEN

The right appliances and kitchen tools can significantly reduce preparation, cooking, and cleanup time and simplify all your kitchen jobs.

Preparing the recipes in this book requires a few extra pieces of equipment in the kitchen. Since the main ingredients are started together and then separated to create the two different variations, you'll need some extra mixing bowls, casserole dishes, and small baking dishes.

I used commercial-quality anodized aluminium nonstick cookware to develop all of the recipes. No added fats or oils are required in food preparation. My recipe testers used a variety of cookware, adapting the recipes using oil or nonstick sprays as needed.

I recommend the following kitchen accessories to speed up preparation and cooking time: a salad spinner, a large colander, a handheld strainer, kitchen shears, cheesecloth, spring-action tongs, a cherry or olive pitter, a small spice grinder or a mortar and pestle, a good selection of knives (including a couple of serrated knives), a knife sharpener, food processors (one medium size, with a four- to six-cup capacity, and one mini processor), an electric mixer, and an electric grill. A microwave oven is required to prepare some of the recipes.

TIME-SAVING PREPARATION TIPS

Reduce preparation time by arranging your cupboards so that you can see all of your spices and seasonings. Many of the following recipes contain several different spices; if you have to empty your cupboards to find a particular spice whenever you need it, you'll be wasting a lot of time. Instead, acquire one or two of those inexpensive tiered shelf inserts that enable you to store goods so all the labels are visible.

By buying prepared products like skinned and boned chicken, deveined shrimp, chopped onions, and minced garlic, you can save time in the kitchen.

With a little preparation, you can use fresh herbs instead of dried. Keep fresh ginger wrapped in plastic in the freezer; you can peel and grate as needed. To store fresh herbs, rinse them well, shake off any excess water, and dry with paper towels. Place the stems into a small glass of water, like fresh-cut flowers. Put a plastic bag over the top, and store in the refrigerator. Chop fresh herbs you use frequently by placing them in a small glass custard cup and mincing them with kitchen scissors. You can then store them in the freezer in plastic bags or mix with water and freeze in ice trays.

You can also freeze unused portions of broth, tomato sauce, tomato paste, and canned chiles in freezer bags for later use.

MENU PLANNING

When planning a menu, always choose foods from the same type of cuisine. Also, make only one recipe that requires a significant amount of cooking and preparation time; the rest of the dishes in the meal should be simple.

Keep a list of favorite recipes on the refrigerator, and keep the required ingredients stocked in the pantry. This way a pleasing meal can be put together in a hurry.

Remember that toddlers may eat only half to a third of an adult serving; by the time children reach ten or twelve years of age, most will eat the same serving size as adults, and teenagers frequently eat more.

But most of all, when deciding what to serve your family, be creative and have fun in the kitchen.

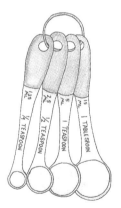

STARTERS

Appetizers are little bites or nibbles that whet the appetite. For children, appetizers can stave off hunger pangs, particularly if the meal is to be served on the late side. Children love to eat with their fingers and, whether served hot or cold, appetizers are the perfect finger food.

While appetizers are not normally part of our weekday evening meals, on weekends, when our schedule is more relaxed, we have time for a family cocktail hour before dinner. It's a wonderful time to share what has been going on and what we have to look forward to in the week ahead. As our children have begun to outgrow their spill-free cups, we've brought out the crystal glasses. Sparkling cider with a tablespoon of black currant syrup makes a delicious children's cocktail. Our children feel grown up sharing this time with us. It also helps teach them how to behave when visiting relatives and friends for dinner.

SAVORY TRIANGLE CRISPS &

PARMESAN TRIANGLE CRISPS

Time to table: 20 minutes   Makes 40 pieces

Oven-baked instead of fried, these triangles have the satisfying crunch of traditional chips. They can be served alone or accompanied by a dip or salsa. For the children, the chips are salted and sprinkled with Parmesan cheese. For the grown-ups, the chips are seasoned with a flavorful blend of Italian seasoning, garlic, paprika, and cheese. The crisps can be made several days ahead and stored in an airtight container.

Olive oil cooking spray
20 square wonton skins, cut in
    half diagonally

$\frac{1}{16}$ teaspoon cayenne
2 tablespoons grated Parmesan
    cheese

GROWN-UPS
1 teaspoon Italian seasoning
$\frac{1}{4}$ teaspoon salt
$\frac{1}{2}$ teaspoon sweet paprika
$\frac{1}{8}$ teaspoon garlic powder

CHILDREN
$\frac{1}{4}$ teaspoon salt
2 tablespoons grated Parmesan
    cheese

Preheat oven to 350 degrees F. Lightly spray a large baking sheet with cooking spray. Arrange the wontons in a single layer and lightly coat with cooking spray. Combine the Italian seasoning, salt, paprika, garlic powder, cayenne, and Parmesan cheese in a small bowl. Sprinkle the mixture over the wontons meant for the grown-ups.

Sprinkle the salt and Parmesan cheese on the wontons for the children.

Bake for 8 minutes or more, until crisp and golden brown. Remove from the oven and allow to cool. Store in an airtight container until ready to serve.

GROWN-UPS
Calories 15; Calories from fat 0
Total fat 0 g; Saturated fat 0 g
Cholesterol 0 mg; Sodium 65 mg
Carbohydrate 2 g; Dietary fiber 0 g
Sugars 0 g; Protein 1 g

CHILDREN
Calories 15; Calories from fat 0
Total fat 0 g; Saturated fat 0 g
Cholesterol 0 mg; Sodium 65 mg
Carbohydrate 2 g; Dietary fiber 0 g
Sugars 0 g; Protein 1 g

Cinnamon Triangle Crisps: Sprinkle the crisps with sugar and cinnamon.
Southwestern Crisps: Sprinkle the crisps with taco seasoning.
Sesame Crisps: Sprinkle the crisps with sesame seeds and salt.
Tortilla Crisps: Substitute flour, whole wheat, or corn tortillas cut into wedges for the wontons.
Pita Crisps: Cut pita bread into wedges and split the wedges in half. Substitute for the wontons.

GARLIC TOASTS &
FANTASY CHEESE TOASTS

Time to table: 20 minutes   Makes 6–8 servings

These toasts are a great accompaniment to cheese or vegetable spreads. For the grown-ups, the bread is toasted, then garlic is rubbed over the toast's rough surface. The toast acts like sandpaper, leaving behind finely grated garlic. For the children, spark their imagination with whimsical shapes that coincide with a special holiday or event. The toasts can be made several hours ahead. Store uncovered at room temperature until ready to serve.

❝*My kids loved the different shapes. We made them over the holidays, and the kids cut them out themselves using Christmas tree and star cookie cutters.*❞

GROWN-UPS
½ French baguette
1–2 garlic cloves, peeled
Olive oil or melted butter
  (optional)

CHILDREN
3 or 4 slices white bread
½ tablespoon melted butter
2 tablespoons grated Parmesan
  cheese

Preheat oven to 350 degrees F.

Cut the French bread on a slight diagonal into 1/2-inch-thick slices and place on a nonstick baking sheet.

Use cookie cutters to cut out shapes from the bread slices, or remove the crusts and cut bread into triangles. Melt the butter in the microwave and brush on one side of the cutouts. Put the Parmesan cheese on a plate and press the buttered side of the bread into the cheese. Shake off excess and place cutouts on the baking sheet cheese side up.

Bake until lightly browned and toasted, 10–15 minutes. Hold the toasted slices in one hand with a pot holder and gently rub the garlic cloves across the top. Lightly brush with olive oil or melted butter, if using. Serve immediately or store for several hours uncovered at room temperature.

GROWN-UPS
Calories 35; Calories from fat 0
Total fat 0 g; Saturated fat 0 g
Cholesterol 0 mg; Sodium 75 mg
Carbohydrate 7 g; Dietary fiber 0 g
Sugars 0 g; Protein 1 g

CHILDREN
Calories 50; Calories from fat 15
Total fat 2 g; Saturated fat 1 g
Cholesterol 5 mg; Sodium 100 mg
Carbohydrate 7 g; Dietary fiber 0 g
Sugars 1 g; Protein 2 g

Raisin Cinnamon Toasts: Use raisin bread instead of plain white bread for the children. Omit the Parmesan cheese and sprinkle with sugar and cinnamon.

SPICY HOT SZECHWAN MEATBALLS &
SWEET ON SWEET MEATBALLS

Time to table: 35 minutes   Makes about 30 meatballs, 15 of each variation

Many of the foods that were popularized in the 50s and 60s are making a comeback. Cocktail meatballs are a perfect example. The children's version, made with grape jelly and ketchup, is sure to appeal to their sweet tooth. The grown-ups' version gets a makeover with spicy Szechwan seasonings—but don't be surprised if you see the grown-ups go for the sweet stuff! The flavor is best if made ahead up to two days in advance and reheated in the microwave just before serving. Have plenty of napkins and toothpicks on hand and a convenient place to dispose of them.

1 pound ground turkey breast or
   extra-lean ground beef
½ cup fresh bread crumbs
⅓ cup skim milk
½ tablespoon Worcestershire sauce
½ garlic clove, minced
2 teaspoons minced onion

GROWN-UPS
½ cup ketchup
2 teaspoons red chili sauce
2 garlic cloves, minced
¼ cup teriyaki sauce
2 teaspoons dark sesame oil

CHILDREN
¼ cup ketchup
¼ cup grape jelly

Preheat oven to 350 degrees F.

Combine the ground turkey, bread crumbs, milk, Worcestershire sauce, garlic, and onion. Form into 1-inch meatballs. Bake on a non-stick baking sheet for 15–20 minutes or until cooked through.

Combine the ketchup, red chili sauce, garlic, teriyaki sauce, and sesame oil in a microwave-safe dish. Microwave at full power for 1–2 minutes. Fold in half of the meatballs until well coated. Serve warm.

In another microwave-safe dish, whisk together the ketchup and grape jelly. Microwave at full power for 1–2 minutes. Whisk again to blend completely. Fold in the remaining meatballs until well coated. Serve warm.

GROWN-UPS
Calories 45; Calories from fat 15
Total fat 1.5 g; Saturated fat 0 g
Cholesterol 10 mg; Sodium 290 mg
Carbohydrate 4 g; Dietary fiber 0 g
Sugars 2 g; Protein 3 g

CHILDREN
Calories 45; Calories from fat 10
Total fat 1 g; Saturated fat 0 g
Cholesterol 10 mg; Sodium 65 mg
Carbohydrate 5 g; Dietary fiber 0 g
Sugars 4 g; Protein 3 g

MINI BAGEL ONION PIZZA &

MINI BAGEL HAM PIZZA

Time to table: 30 minutes   **Makes 18 pieces**

Pizza is one of America's favorite foods. For the grown-ups, bagels are topped with sweet onions, black olives, and anchovies for those with a sense of adventure. Use sweet onions, like Maui, Vidalia, or Walla Walla. If these are unavailable, use yellow onions with a pinch of sugar. For the children, bagels are topped with their favorite pizza toppings. These pizzas can be assembled several days ahead and refrigerated until ready to bake.

Anytime pizza is involved, I know that I'll have no problems getting my kids to eat. I've made the mini pizzas for lunch and dinner, too.

9 plain mini bagels, sliced in half
1½ cups low-fat or regular
   mozzarella cheese, about 4
   ounces

5 or 6 chopped Greek olives or
   black olives
5–6 anchovy fillets, drained and
   chopped (optional)

GROWN-UPS
1 large sweet onion, thinly sliced,
   about ½ pound
2 tablespoons dry white wine

CHILDREN
½ cup pizza or spaghetti sauce
3–4 ounces diced low-fat ham,
   sausage, or Canadian bacon

Preheat oven to 350 degrees F.

For the grown-ups, heat a large nonstick skillet over medium-high heat for 2 minutes. Add onion and stir for 2–3 minutes. Add the wine and olives. Reduce heat to low, cover, and simmer for 10 minutes, stirring occasionally. Add more wine if the pan goes dry. Remove the cover and allow the liquid to evaporate while stirring.

Place a thin layer of mozzarella on half of the mini bagels. Top with the onion mixture and sprinkle with anchovies, if desired. Place the bagels on a nonstick baking sheet.

Spread the pizza sauce on the remaining bagels. Top with a layer of cheese and ham. Place the bagels on the baking sheet.

Bake until the cheese is melted, 8–10 minutes.

Note: Pizza sauce comes in convenient squeezable bottles. Just squeeze out the amount needed and refrigerate the rest.

GROWN-UPS	CHILDREN
Calories 100; Calories from fat 20	Calories 120; Calories from fat 30
Total fat 2 g; Saturated fat 1 g	Total fat 3.5 g; Saturated fat 1.5 g
Cholesterol 5 mg; Sodium 200 mg	Cholesterol 10 mg; Sodium 430 mg
Carbohydrate 15 g; Dietary fiber 1 g	Carbohydrate 15 g; Dietary fiber 0 g
Sugars 2 g; Protein 5 g	Sugars 2 g; Protein 8 g

BRUSCHETTA WITH SUN-DRIED
TOMATO TAPENADE & BRUSCHETTA
WITH APPLE-RAISIN TAPENADE

Time to table: 20 minutes   Makes 16–18 bruschetta

❝*I've served this appetizer at many dinner parties to rave reviews from both adults and children. I like having the two different variations.*❞

Bruschetta is the original garlic bread. It is easy to prepare under the broiler or on the grill. For the grown-ups, the bruschetta is topped with a flavorful tapenade made from sun-dried tomatoes. For the children, a sweet tapenade is made from raisins and dried apples. To serve, place it in a decorative bowl surrounded by bruschetta. They can be made several days in advance. The bruschetta can be made several hours ahead and stored uncovered at room temperature until ready to serve.

1 French baguette
1 or 2 garlic cloves as needed
Melted butter (optional)

GROWN-UPS
Sun-Dried Tomato Tapenade
(recipe follows)

CHILDREN
Apple-Raisin Tapenade (recipe
follows)

Heat oven to broil. Cut the bread into 1/2-inch diagonal slices. Place the slices on a broiling pan and toast for a few minutes on each side until browned. (Watch carefully so that the toasts do not burn.) Rub the garlic cloves over the bruschetta for the grown-ups. Brush the bruschetta for the children with melted butter, if desired.

SUN-DRIED TOMATO TAPENADE

2 cloves garlic, peeled
1 green onion
1 tablespoon capers, rinsed
1 cup oil-packed sun-dried
* tomatoes, rinsed and well*
* drained*

1 teaspoon dried oregano
2 teaspoons balsamic vinegar
2 tablespoons fresh lemon juice
Salt to taste

Add the garlic, green onion, and capers to the bowl of a food processor. Process until chopped. Add the tomatoes, oregano, balsamic vinegar, lemon juice, and salt. Process until well chopped and blended. Chill for several hours for best flavor.

APPLE-RAISIN TAPENADE

1 cup dried apple
¼ cup apple juice
2 tablespoons raisins or dried
   cranberries

1 tablespoon brown sugar
½ tablespoon fresh lemon
   juice
½ teaspoon ground cinnamon

Add the apple, apple juice, raisins, brown sugar, lemon juice, and cinnamon to a food processor and process until well chopped. Chill for several hours for best flavor.

GROWN-UPS
Calories 50; Calories from fat 5
Total fat 0.5 g; Saturated fat 0 g
Cholesterol 0 mg; Sodium 190 mg
Carbohydrate 100 g; Dietary fiber 1 g
Sugars 3 g; Protein 2 g

CHILDREN
Calories 60; Calories from fat 0
Total fat 0 g; Saturated fat 0 g
Cholesterol 0 mg; Sodium 70 mg
Carbohydrate 13 g; Dietary fiber 1 g
Sugars 7 g; Protein 1 g

MINI SUN-DRIED TOMATO
CHEESECAKES & MINI HAM AND
CHEESECAKES

Time to table: 35 minutes   **Makes 36 cheesecakes**

These savory little cheesecakes make attractive appetizers. For the grown-ups, the cheesecakes are flavored with sun-dried tomatoes and rosemary. Bacon and Cheddar cheese are more to the kids' liking. The cheesecakes can be made several days ahead and stored in the refrigerator until ready to serve. Have plenty of napkins on hand and a convenient place to dispose of the wrappers.

❝My daughter especially loved these mini cheesecakes. I keep them in the freezer and reheat for a quick snack after school. The kids also like them for brunch.❞

1 15-ounce carton fat-free ricotta cheese
1 8-ounce package light cream cheese or Neufchâtel, softened
2 egg whites
¼ cup grated Parmesan cheese
¼ teaspoon salt

GROWN-UPS
¼ cup oil-packed sun-dried tomatoes, rinsed and chopped

2 garlic cloves, minced
½ tablespoon crumbled dried rosemary

CHILDREN
4 slices chopped Canadian bacon
¼ cup finely grated Cheddar cheese, reduced fat or regular

Preheat oven to 350 degrees F. Line three mini muffin trays with muffin cups.

Mix together the ricotta cheese, cream cheese, egg whites, Parmesan cheese, and salt in a 2-quart measuring bowl. Transfer half of the mixture to another bowl.

Fold in the tomatoes, garlic, and rosemary to half of the mixture. Divide this mixture evenly into eighteen of the muffin cups.

Fold the ham and cheese into the other half of the mixture. Spoon into the remaining muffin cups.

Bake for 25 minutes. The centers will not be set but will firm up when chilled. Let cool to room temperature, cover, and chill until ready to serve.

GROWN-UPS
Calories 30; Calories from fat 10
Total fat 1.5 g; Saturated fat 1 g
Cholesterol 5 mg; Sodium 75 mg
Carbohydrate 2 g; Dietary fiber 0 g
Sugars 1 g; Protein 2 g

CHILDREN
Calories 35; Calories from fat 15
Total fat 2 g; Saturated fat 1 g
Cholesterol 5 mg; Sodium 140 mg
Carbohydrate 1 g; Dietary fiber 0 g
Sugars 1 g; Protein 2 g

Mini Roasted Red-Pepper Cheesecakes: Substitute 1/4 cup chopped roasted red peppers for the sun-dried tomatoes.

SPICY BUFFALO SHRIMP &
SWEET BUFFALO SHRIMP

Time to table: 20 minutes   Makes 36 servings, 18 of each variation

The recipe is a takeoff on the ever-popular Buffalo wings, with shrimp substituting for chicken. For the children, who are sensitive to hot spices, the sauce is toned down quite a bit, but for the grown-ups the sauce can be as spicy as you like. The shrimp cook in a matter of minutes. The sauces will keep for several days in the refrigerator. Pour the sauces over the shrimp and pop into the oven.

Great and easy. I split the recipe, using shrimp for the adults and chicken wings for the kids. They were perfectly happy.

Vegetable cooking spray
36 large shrimp, peeled and
    deveined
¼ cup packed dark brown sugar
¼ cup chopped onion
3 or 4 garlic cloves, minced fine
⅓ cup cider vinegar

¼ cup water
¼ cup ketchup
1 tablespoon Worcestershire sauce

GROWN-UPS
1–2 teaspoons red chili sauce
¼ teaspoon cayenne

Preheat oven to 400 degrees F. Lightly spray two small baking dishes with vegetable cooking spray, and place half of the shrimp in each.

Combine the brown sugar, onion, garlic, cider vinegar, water, ketchup, and Worcestershire in a saucepan. Bring to a boil, reduce heat, and cook for 10 minutes, stirring occasionally. Pour half of the mixture over the shrimp for the children, stirring to combine.

Stir the red chili sauce and cayenne into the remaining sauce and pour over the shrimp for the grown-ups, stirring to combine.

Place the baking dishes in the oven and bake for 6–8 minutes until cooked through. Serve warm or chilled.

GROWN-UPS
Calories 15; Calories from fat 0
Total fat 0 g; Saturated fat 0 g
Cholesterol 10 mg; Sodium 40 mg
Carbohydrate 2 g; Dietary fiber 0 g
Sugars 1 g; Protein 1 g

CHILDREN
Calories 15; Calories from fat 0
Total fat 0 g; Saturated fat 0 g
Cholesterol 10 mg; Sodium 40 mg
Carbohydrate 2 g; Dietary fiber 0 g
Sugars 2 g; Protein 1 g

Spicy Chicken Wings: Substitute chicken wings or chicken drumettes for the shrimp.

SPICY CRAB QUESADILLAS &
CHEESY CRAB QUESADILLAS

Time to table: about 20 minutes   **Makes 16 wedges, 8 of each variation**

These tasty tortilla wedges are crisp on the outside and creamy on the inside. Arrange attractively on a serving platter accompanied by sour cream, salsa, and sliced jalapeño peppers. When I use fat-free sour cream, I stir in a few tablespoons of taco seasoning to boost the flavor. For best flavor use fresh real crabmeat. Serve warm right out of the oven.

> *Our kids were just as happy with plain cheese quesadillas, which was just as well—since it left more crab for us.*

Olive oil cooking spray
4 ounces fresh cooked
    crabmeat
1 cup shredded Monterey Jack
    or Cheddar cheese, reduced-fat
    or regular, about 4 ounces
8 6-inch flour tortillas

Optional garnish: cilantro sprigs,
    low-fat sour cream, salsa, and
    chopped jalapeño peppers

GROWN-UPS
1 green onion, sliced thin
¼ cup chopped fresh cilantro
2 tablespoons salsa

Preheat oven to 375 degrees F. Lightly coat a large baking sheet with cooking spray.

Mix together the crabmeat and cheese. Spread half of the mixture on two tortillas to within 3/4 inch of the edges. Cover each with another tortilla and transfer to the baking sheet. Lightly spray the top with cooking spray.

Fold in the green onion and cilantro to the remaining crab mixture. Spread on two tortillas to within 3/4 inch of the edges. Sprinkle with salsa and top with the remaining tortillas. Transfer to the baking sheet and lightly spray with cooking spray.

Bake in preheated oven for 10 minutes until the cheese is melted. Slide the tortillas onto a cutting board and cut into quarters. Arrange on a serving platter with fresh cilantro. Place the sour cream, salsa, and jalapeños in small bowls with spoons for serving.

GROWN-UPS
Calories 100; Calories from fat 15
Total fat 2 g; Saturated fat 1 g
Cholesterol 10 mg; Sodium 260 mg
Carbohydrate 14g; Dietary fiber 0 g
Sugars 0 g; Protein 6 g

CHILDREN
Calories 100; Calories from fat 150
Total fat 2 g; Saturated fat 1 g
Cholesterol 10 mg; Sodium 250 mg
Carbohydrate 14 g; Dietary fiber 0 g
Sugars 0 g; Protein 6 g

DILL NEW POTATO SKINS & HAM AND CHEDDAR NEW POTATO SKINS

Time to table: about 30 minutes   Makes 20 servings, 10 of each variation

Very tasty. One of my children liked the potatoes with just cheese. The others like the adult variation better.

Potato skins were all the rage some fifteen years ago, but loaded with bacon and Cheddar cheese they were hardly a healthy choice. In recent years, potato skins are making a comeback with lighter ingredients. For the children, Cheddar cheese and Canadian bacon are used to flavor the skins. For the grown-ups, ranch-style sour cream seasoned with dill and a light sprinkle of Cheddar cheese is used. The potato skins are best served hot right out of the oven. You can prepare the potatoes and sour-cream filling up to two days in advance. Assemble the potato skins and heat for 10–15 minutes before serving. Use the tiny new potatoes; if larger potatoes are used, increase the baking time to about twenty minutes.

10 small new potatoes, about 2 inches in diameter	Salt and pepper to taste Chopped dill for garnish

GROWN-UPS	CHILDREN
⅓ cup sour cream, fat-free, low-fat, or regular	Salt to taste
1 teaspoon ranch-style salad dressing mix	4 slices Canadian bacon, finely diced
1 tablespoon chopped fresh dill	¼ cup grated reduced-fat or regular Cheddar cheese

Preheat oven to 450 degrees F. Wash and scrub the potatoes. Prick the skins with a knife. Microwave at full power for 2 minutes. Reduce power setting to "bake" and microwave for 5 minutes more. Place in the conventional oven for 10 minutes until the skins are crisp and the centers are soft. Remove from the oven and slice in half. Holding the potatoes with a pot holder, scoop out the centers, leaving a ¼-inch shell. (Save the potato centers as a soup thickener for creamed soups or fold into mashed potatoes. Place in a freezer bag and store in the refrigerator until ready to use.)

While the potatoes are cooking, mix together the sour cream, ranch dressing, and dill. Let stand for about 10 minutes. Season the potato skins for the grown-ups with salt and pepper. Spoon the sour cream mixture into the skins and place on a baking sheet.

Season the potato skins for the children with salt. Evenly distribute the Canadian bacon and Cheddar cheese into the skins and place on the baking sheet.

Bake the stuffed skins for 5–7 minutes until heated through. Garnish the skins for the grown-ups with chopped dill. Serve immediately.

GROWN-UPS
Calories 45; Calories from fat 0
Total fat 0 g; Saturated fat 0 g
Cholesterol 0 mg; Sodium 130 mg
Carbohydrate 10 g; Dietary fiber 0 g
Sugars 1 g; Protein 2 g

CHILDREN
Calories 45; Calories from fat 0
Total fat 0 g; Saturated fat 0 g
Cholesterol 5 mg; Sodium 60 mg
Carbohydrate 8 g; Dietary fiber 0 g
Sugars 1 g; Protein 4 g

SALADS

Kids' tastes vary considerably when it comes to eating vegetables. Some children prefer the milder flavor of iceberg lettuce to the more flavorful and sometimes slightly bitter dark-green varieties of lettuce. The great thing about salads is that they can be made with an almost endless variety of fruits, vegetables, and greens.

Traditional green salads are often too boring to interest children in eating them. Try mixing fresh fruit with various greens for a new approach. My children rarely eat salads in which everything is mixed together. Instead, I serve the salad fixings grouped separately on the serving platter. Cherry tomatoes, wedges of cucumber, and pieces of fruit on skewers are also a delightful treat. When I am feeling particularly creative, I'll make a face out of the vegetables on the plate. In the summer we often forgo the formality of green salads for a platter of fresh fruit. Melon slices, a bowl of fresh strawberries, or sliced peaches make a wonderful substitute, and the children seldom have to be coaxed into eating them.

Make a batch of your family's favorite salad dressing to keep on hand for occasions when preparation time is limited. I keep a supply of my children's favorite store-bought dressings in the pantry, too. Creamy Italian, traditional Italian, and ranch dressings are their favorites, since many vinegar-based dressings tend to be too sour for kids. Serve the dressings on the side in small bowls.

I've found that many fat-free store-bought dressings can ruin a perfectly good salad. I prefer to make my own. Most of the dressings in this book use a scant half tablespoon of oil and are rather tart. If you are not accustomed to a low-fat diet, use more oil until your taste buds become accustomed to the sharper taste of lower-fat salad dressings. I use puréed fruit, vegetables, buttermilk, or cheese to provide extra body in these low-fat dressings.

MIXED CITRUS SALAD &

ORANGE CUCUMBER SALAD

Time to table: 20 minutes   Serves 2 adults and 2 or 3 children

For special occasions, use fresh orange and grapefruit; when time is limited, use canned mandarin oranges and grapefruit. For my children, who aren't big salad eaters, I serve cucumber wedges and mandarin oranges on skewers and leave it at that.

> ❝I enjoyed the citrus in this salad for a nice
> change from the usual vegetables.❞

4–5 cups torn red leaf lettuce,
   rinsed and spun dry
1 large orange
1 grapefruit

GROWN-UPS
1 or 2 very thin slices of red onion
¼ cup thin slices red bell pepper

Orange Ginger Vinaigrette (recipe
   follows)

CHILDREN
½ cucumber, peeled and cut into
   wedges
¼ cup ranch or other favorite
   dressing, low-fat or regular

Tear the lettuce into bite-size pieces and arrange on individual salad plates. Cut the top and bottom off the orange and grapefruit. With a sharp knife, remove the rind, following the contour of the fruit. Remove the sections by sliding a sharp knife next to the membrane on both sides of each section. Remove any visible seeds. Place on the salads, omitting from the children's if not to their liking.

Arrange the onions and red peppers on the salads for the grown-ups. Serve with Orange Ginger Vinaigrette.

Arrange the cucumbers on the salads for the children. Serve with ranch or other favorite dressing.

ORANGE GINGER VINAIGRETTE

½ tablespoon extra-virgin olive oil
2 tablespoons strained applesauce
(baby food)
1 tablespoon orange juice
concentrate
2 tablespoons rice vinegar

1 medium clove garlic, minced
½ teaspoon fresh grated ginger or
¼ teaspoon powdered ginger
⅛ teaspoon white pepper
¼ teaspoon ground cumin
(optional)

Mix together the olive oil and applesauce. Stir in the orange juice concentrate, rice vinegar, garlic, ginger, white pepper, and cumin (if using) until well mixed.

GROWN-UPS
Calories 120; Calories from fat 35
Total fat 4 g; Saturated fat 0.5 g
Cholesterol 0 mg; Sodium 320 mg
Carbohydrate 22 g; Dietary fiber 4 g
Sugars 16 g; Protein 3 g

CHILDREN
Calories 80; Calories from fat 35
Total fat 3.5 g; Saturated fat 0 g
Cholesterol 0 mg; Sodium 125 mg
Carbohydrate 10 g; Dietary fiber 2 g
Sugars 6 g; Protein 2 g

MIXED BERRY SALAD WITH ROSEMARY RASPBERRY VINAIGRETTE & MIXED BERRY SALAD WITH CREAMY RASPBERRY DRESSING

Time to table: 15 minutes   Serves 2 adults and 2 or 3 children

The delightful combination of sweet and savory flavors work beautifully in this unusual pairing of salad greens with fresh summer berries. Mixed baby greens or mesclun have a slightly bitter, peppery flavor that is offset by the sweetness of the raspberries and blackberries. A continuation of the theme pairs raspberry flavored vinegar with rosemary in a perfectly balanced vinaigrette. For the children, a sweet, creamy raspberry dressing is the perfect finish.

4–5 cups mixed salad greens,
  rinsed and spun dry
½ cup raspberries, rinsed and
  drained
½ cup blackberries, rinsed and
  drained

GROWN-UPS
2 tablespoons chopped red onion

Rosemary Raspberry Vinaigrette
  (recipe follows)

CHILDREN
Creamy Raspberry Dressing
  (recipe follows)

**❝This was just fabulous. My children are not big salad
eaters but they loved the fresh berries.❞**

Arrange the salad greens on individual plates. Scatter the berries on
the salads.

Scatter the red onion on the salads for the grown-ups and serve with
Raspberry Vinaigrette.

Serve the salads for the children with Creamy Raspberry Dressing.

ROSEMARY RASPBERRY VINAIGRETTE

1 garlic clove, peeled
¼ shallot, peeled
2 tablespoons strained applesauce
  (baby food)
1 teaspoon honey Dijon mustard

½ tablespoon extra-virgin olive oil
2 tablespoons raspberry vinegar
⅛ teaspoon salt
½ teaspoon sugar
½ teaspoon dried rosemary

Process the garlic and shallot until well chopped. Add the applesauce, mustard, olive oil, raspberry vinegar, salt, sugar, and rosemary.
Process until well blended and smooth. Let stand until ready to serve.

CREAMY RASPBERRY DRESSING

¼ cup mayonnaise, low-fat or
regular

½ tablespoon raspberry vinegar
1 teaspoon sugar

Mix together the mayonnaise, vinegar, and sugar. Let stand until ready to serve.

GROWN-UPS
Calories 110; Calories from fat 40
Total fat 4.5 g; Saturated fat 0.5 g
Cholesterol 0 mg; Sodium 230 mg
Carbohydrate 18 g; Dietary fiber 6 g
Sugars 8 g; Protein 3 g

CHILDREN
Calories 60; Calories from fat 10
Total fat 1 g; Saturated fat 0 g
Cholesterol 0 mg; Sodium 120 mg
Carbohydrate 11 g; Dietary fiber 3 g
Sugars 7 g; Protein 1 g

GORGONZOLA PEAR AND PECAN
SALAD & RANCH PEAR
AND PECAN SALAD

Time to table: 20 minutes   Serves 2 adults and 2 or 3 children

This is a wonderful salad to make in the winter, when pears and nuts are in season. The butter lettuce has a delicate, almost sweet flavor that makes the perfect base for the salad. Gorgonzola cheese and buttermilk combine to make a creamy, rich dressing that blends all the flavors together.

❝Everyone in our family enjoyed this salad. I don't often use fruit or nuts in salads, so it was a nice change from the usual. I added red seedless grapes at the last minute, which added more color. I'll make this dressing again and again.❞

4–5 cups butter lettuce, rinsed and
   spun dry
2 firm ripe Bartlett pears, cut into
   quarters, cored and sliced thin
2 tablespoons chopped pecans,
   toasted

GROWN-UPS
1 or 2 green onions, sliced, green
   part only
Creamy Gorgonzola Dressing
   (recipe follows)

CHILDREN
¼ cup ranch or other favorite
   dressing, low-fat or regular

Arrange the salad greens on separate plates. Divide the pears among the plates. Scatter the pecans over the pears.

Arrange the green onion on the salads for the grown-ups and serve with Creamy Gorgonzola Dressing.

For the children, serve the salads with ranch or other favorite dressing.

CREAMY GORGONZOLA DRESSING

1 small garlic clove, peeled
¼ cup low-fat buttermilk or low-
   fat milk
2 tablespoons crumbled
   Gorgonzola or bleu cheese

½ teaspoon red wine vinegar
⅛ teaspoon salt
Freshly ground black pepper
   to taste

Chop the garlic in a mini food processor. Add the buttermilk, Gorgonzola, vinegar, and salt. Process until smooth. Season to taste with freshly ground black pepper.

GROWN-UPS
Calories 130; Calories from fat 50
Total fat 6 g; Saturated fat 2 g
Cholesterol 5 mg; Sodium 300 mg
Carbohydrate 17 g; Dietary fiber 3 g
Sugars 12 g; Protein 4 g

CHILDREN
Calories 100; Calories from fat 50
Total fat 5 g; Saturated fat 0 g
Cholesterol 0 mg; Sodium 125 mg
Carbohydrate 11 g; Dietary fiber 2 g
Sugars 6 g; Protein 2 g

ORANGE GINGER RED CABBAGE SLAW
& APPLE AND RED CABBAGE SLAW

Time to table: 20 minutes   Serves 2 or 3 adults and 3 or 4 children

Orange and ginger provide a touch of the Orient in this crunchy salad made with red cabbage and apples. The apples temper the sharpness of cabbage while the light citrus dressing brings the flavors together. Use a large-capacity food processor to make short work of shredding the cabbage and apple. The slaw is ready in about twenty minutes, but the flavors are more pronounced if allowed to blend for an hour or more.

> ❝*I never made slaw without mayonnaise before. This was a nice change.*❞

1 pound red cabbage, about half of
  a small cabbage
1 Golden Delicious apple, rinsed,
  quartered, and cored

GROWN-UPS
1 green onion, sliced thin
2 tablespoons seasoned rice vinegar
2 tablespoons orange juice
  concentrate

½ teaspoon grated orange zest
½ teaspoon grated fresh ginger
⅛ teaspoon salt

CHILDREN
½ cup salad dressing or
  mayonnaise, reduced-fat or
  regular
1 teaspoon sugar
⅛ teaspoon salt

Remove the core of the cabbage and discard. Cut the cabbage into pieces that will fit into the feeder tube of a food processor. Use the shredding disk of the food processor to shred the cabbage. (You should have about 4 cups.) Do this in batches if the food processor is not large enough to hold all the cabbage at once. Transfer to a large bowl. Use the grating disk of the processor to grate the apple and transfer to the bowl. Toss the cabbage and apple together. Transfer half of the mixture to another bowl.

For the grown-ups, stir in the green onion. Combine the rice vinegar, orange juice concentrate, orange zest, ginger, and salt in a small bowl. Pour over the slaw and stir to blend.

For the children, mix the salad dressing, sugar, and salt in a small bowl. Pour over the slaw and stir to blend.

GROWN-UPS
Calories 50; Calories from fat 0
Total fat 0 g; Saturated fat 0 g
Cholesterol 0 mg; Sodium 460 mg
Carbohydrate 13 g; Dietary fiber 3 g
Sugars 11 g; Protein 1 g

CHILDREN
Calories 70; Calories from fat 35
Total fat 4 g; Saturated fat 2 g
Cholesterol 10 mg; Sodium 160 mg
Carbohydrate 7 g; Dietary fiber 1 g
Sugars 4 g; Protein 1 g

CITRUS JICAMA SLAW
& ITALIAN JICAMA SLAW

Time to table: 20 minutes   **Serves 2 adults and 2 or 3 children**

Jicama (pronounced hee-kah-mah) looks like a cross between a large onion and a knobby potato with dark brown skin. The thin skin peels off easily, revealing snowy white flesh with a texture similar to water chestnut. The mild, sweet, and nutty flavor is unlike any other. Carrots are a natural complement in both texture and color. For the grown-ups, orange, lemon, and lime juice make the base of the sweet dressing. Basil sliced into thin strips adds color and a fresh, fruity flavor. If desired, add jalapeños for a little extra kick. For the children, you may want to offer carrot and jicama sticks on a serving platter with their favorite dressing on the side.

1 pound jicama, peeled and cut
    into pieces
2 carrots, trimmed and peeled

Basil Citrus Dressing (recipe
    follows)
Salt and pepper to taste

GROWN-UPS
1 teaspoon minced (canned or
    jarred) jalapeño peppers
    (optional)

CHILDREN
Creamy Italian dressing or
    mayonnaise, low-fat or regular
Salt to taste

Grate the jicama and carrots in a food processor. Divide in half and transfer to two bowls.

Stir the jalapeño, if using, and Basil Citrus Dressing into the adults' portion. Season with salt and pepper.

Stir the creamy Italian dressing or mayonnaise into the children's portion. Season with salt.

BASIL CITRUS DRESSING

2 tablespoons orange juice
   concentrate
2 tablespoons lime juice
2 tablespoons lemon juice
1 teaspoon sugar

⅛ teaspoon salt
1 garlic clove, minced
4 or 5 fresh basil leaves, cut into
   very thin strips

Mix the orange juice concentrate, lime juice, lemon juice, sugar, and salt together. Stir in the garlic and basil.

GROWN-UPS
Calories 80; Calories from fat 0
Total fat 0 g; Saturated fat 0 g
Cholesterol 0 mg; Sodium 490 mg
Carbohydrate 19 g; Dietary fiber 5 g
Sugars 13 g; Protein 2 g

CHILDREN
Calories 70; Calories from fat 25
Total fat 3 g; Saturated fat 0.5 g
Cholesterol 0 mg; Sodium 210 mg
Carbohydrate 12 g; Dietary fiber 4 g
Sugars 3 g; Protein 1 g

ORANGE CURRY CARROT SLAW &

PINEAPPLE RAISIN CARROT SLAW

Time to table: 20 minutes   **Serves 2 adults and 2 or 3 children**

Carrots, raisins, and pineapple are joined together in an unusual blend of flavors. The dressing is seasoned with curry, mango chutney, and orange. For children who do not like their foods mixed together, place carrot sticks, pineapple chunks, and raisins on a salad plate.

❝*I like curry a lot, and so does my husband. We were pleasantly surprised.*❞

5–6 medium-size carrots, trimmed
    and peeled, about 1¼ pounds
¼ cup raisins
1 8-ounce can crushed pineapple,
    drained

GROWN-UPS
1 teaspoon curry powder
    (preferably Madras Curry)
2 teaspoons orange juice
    concentrate

¼ cup low-fat mayonnaise
⅛ teaspoon salt
2 tablespoons mango chutney,
    chopped if very chunky

CHILDREN
¼ cup salad dressing or
    mayonnaise, low-fat or regular
⅛ teaspoon salt

Grate the carrots in a food processor. Transfer to a large bowl. Stir in the raisins and pineapple. Transfer half to another bowl.

For the grown-ups, toast the curry powder in a dry skillet or saucepan over medium-high heat for 1–2 minutes, shaking the pan frequently. In a small bowl, combine the curry powder, orange juice concentrate, mayonnaise, salt, and chutney. Fold into the grown-ups' portion.

Fold the mayonnaise and salt into the children's portion.

GROWN-UPS
Calories 160; Calories from fat 5
Total fat 0.5 g; Saturated fat 0 g
Cholesterol 0 mg; Sodium 430 mg
Carbohydrate 38 g; Dietary fiber 5 g
Sugars 29 g; Protein 2 g

CHILDREN
Calories 60; Calories from fat 0
Total fat 0 g; Saturated fat 0 g
Cholesterol 0 mg; Sodium 160 mg
Carbohydrate 16 g; Dietary fiber 2 g
Sugars 12 g; Protein 1 g

FENNEL WALDORF SALAD
& APPLE WALDORF SALAD

Time to table: 20 minutes   Serves 2 adults and 2 to 4 children

The original Waldorf salad, made with apples, celery, and mayonnaise, was created at the Waldorf-Astoria Hotel in the late 1800s. In my updated version, celery is replaced by fennel, which has the same texture but adds a slightly sweet and mild licorice flavor. Fresh fennel can be found in the produce section and is often labeled *anise* or *sweet anise*. If the stalks are attached, it looks similar to celery but with a bulbous root end and feathery leaves. The leaves can be used as a fresh herb, much like dill. For the children, the salad is prepared along traditional lines with celery; however, some children might prefer apple wedges and celery sticks instead of everything mixed together.

> ❞We really like the fennel. I've seen it before
> at the supermarket but never knew what it was.
> I wasn't too sure that my kids would try the salad
> all mixed together so I gave them apple wedges
> and celery sticks, which are familiar to them, and
> a little cup of vanilla yogurt.❞

3 medium-size Golden Delicious
    apples, about 1¼ pounds
2 tablespoons fresh lemon juice
Walnut Yogurt Dressing (recipe
    follows)

GROWN-UPS
1 cup chopped fennel or celery
1 tablespoon chopped fennel leaves

CHILDREN
1 cup chopped celery

Rinse the apples, cut into quarters, and remove the core. Cut each quarter in half and slice into even-size pieces. Place the apples into a large mixing bowl and toss with lemon juice to keep from browning. Fold in the Walnut Yogurt Dressing. Transfer half to another dish.

Fold the fennel and chopped fennel leaves into the salad for the grown-ups. Fold the celery into the salad for the children.

Can be served immediately but tastes better if chilled for several hours to allow the flavors to blend.

WALNUT YOGURT DRESSING

½ cup nonfat vanilla yogurt
¼ cup low-fat mayonnaise
1 teaspoon walnut extract

2 tablespoons chopped walnuts,
  toasted
¼ teaspoon salt

In a small bowl, combine the vanilla yogurt, low-fat mayonnaise, walnut extract, walnuts, and salt.

GROWN-UPS
Calories 210; Calories from fat 50
Total fat 6 g; Saturated fat 1 g
Cholesterol 5 mg; Sodium 310 mg
Carbohydrate 32 g; Dietary fiber 4 g
Sugars 22 g; Protein 6 g

CHILDREN
Calories 170; Calories from fat 50
Total fat 6 g; Saturated fat 1.5 g
Cholesterol 15 mg; Sodium 130 mg
Carbohydrate 18 g; Dietary fiber 2 g
Sugars 14 g; Protein 3 g

RASPBERRY WALNUT CARROT SALAD
& PINEAPPLE CARROT SALAD

Time to table: 20 mintues   **Serves 2 adults and 2 or 3 children**

An unusual dressing made with raspberry vinegar, walnut oil, and sweet hot mustard brings out the natural sweetness of the carrots.

❝I was surprised by how good this tasted. I'm familiar with raisins and mayonnaise in carrot slaw. This was a refreshing change.❞

5–6 medium-size carrots,
  peeled and trimmed, about 1¼
  pounds

GROWN-UPS
Raspberry Walnut Vinaigrette
  (receipe follows)
Salt and pepper to taste

2 tablespoons chopped flat-leaf
  parsley

CHILDREN
1 8-ounce can crushed pineapple,
  drained
¼ cup low-fat or regular
  mayonnaise

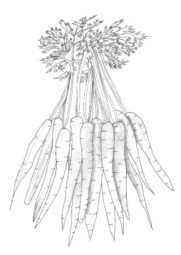

Grate the carrots in a food processor. You should have about 3 to 4 cups. Divide in half and transfer to two separate bowls.

Fold the crushed pineapple and mayonnaise into the children's portion. Chill until ready to serve.

Fold the Raspberry Walnut Vinaigrette into the grown-ups' portion. Season with salt and pepper. Chill until ready to serve. Fold in the parsley just before serving.

Raspberry Walnut Vinaigrette

2 teaspoons sweet hot mustard
½ tablespoon walnut oil
2 tablespoons raspberry vinegar
2 tablespoons strained applesauce
    (baby food)

1 garlic clove, minced
½ teaspoon sugar
¼ teaspoon salt

Whisk together the mustard and walnut oil. Stir in the vinegar, applesauce, garlic, sugar, and salt.

GROWN-UPS
Calories 130; Calories from fat 60
Total fat 7 g; Saturated fat 0.5 g
Cholesterol 0 mg; Sodium 420 mg
Carbohydrate 17 g; Dietary fiber 4 g
Sugars 12 g; Protein 1 g

CHILDREN
Calories 100; Calories from fat 20
Total fat 2 g; Saturated fat 1 g
Cholesterol 10 mg; Sodium 95 mg
Carbohydrate 16 g; Dietary fiber 3 g
Sugars 11 g; Protein 1 g

HONEY MUSTARD MIXED BEAN SALAD
& ITALIAN MIXED BEAN SALAD

Time to table: 20 minutes   Serves 2 adults and 2 or 3 children

The yellow and green beans provide a nice visual contrast, although using just one or the other is fine. Red peppers and onions add color and crunch to the salad. For the grown-ups, the sweet hot-mustard dressing is easy to make. For the children, serve the dressing on the side.

❝For my kids, I just placed the whole beans on salad plates with small bowls of salad dressing. They ate them with their fingers.❞

½ pound yellow wax beans, rinsed and trimmed
¾ pound green beans, rinsed and trimmed

GROWN-UPS
¼ cup chopped red onions
¼ cup finely diced red peppers
Honey Mustard Dressing (recipe follows)

Salt and freshly ground black pepper to taste

CHILDREN
2–3 tablespoons bottled Italian dressing, low-fat or regular
Salt to taste

Bring 2 quarts of water to a boil. Add the beans and cook until crisp tender, about 2–3 minutes. Drain and cover with ice water for about 5 minutes. Drain again and pat dry with paper towels. Cut the beans into 2-inch pieces. Divide in half and transfer to two separate bowls.

Fold the red onions and red peppers into the portion for the grown-ups. Toss with the Honey Mustard Dressing. Season with salt and pepper.

Toss the children's portion with Italian dressing. Season with salt.

HONEY MUSTARD DRESSING

2 tablespoons sweet hot mustard *1 clove garlic, minced*
1 tablespoon honey *1–2 teaspoons rice vinegar*

Combine the sweet hot mustard, honey, and garlic in a small bowl. Stir in enough rice vinegar to reach the consistency of salad dressing.

GROWN-UPS
Calories 100; Calories from fat 0
Total fat 0 g; Saturated fat 0 g
Cholesterol 0 mg; Sodium 420 mg
Carbohydrate 22 g; Dietary fiber 4 g
Sugars 14 g; Protein 3 g

CHILDREN
Calories 70; Calories from fat 45
Total fat 5 g; Saturated fat 0.5 g
Cholesterol 0 mg; Sodium 80 mg
Carbohydrate 80 g; Dietary fiber 3 g
Sugars 3 g; Protein 2 g

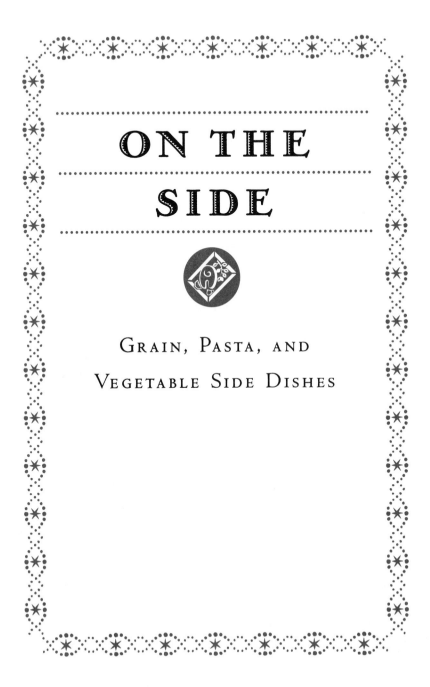

ON THE SIDE

Grain, Pasta, and
Vegetable Side Dishes

RICE, GRAINS, AND PASTA

R ice, grains, and pasta make perfect side dishes. The secret to adapting these recipes to children's tastes is to add plenty of fresh herbs to the adult portions at the end of the cooking process. The children's portions can be seasoned simply or customized to their liking.

My favorite side dishes include basmati rice, quinoa, couscous, polenta, bulgur wheat, and pastas, most of which can be found in the rice and grain or pasta section of your regular supermarket.

Basmati rice has a perfumy, nutty flavor and aroma that appeals to adults and children. It has been grown in the foothills of the Himalayas for thousands of years, and it is a staple of East Indian cuisine. Once considered an exotic food, it can now be found in many American supermarkets. Basmati rice cooks in about fifteen minutes on the stove or in the microwave. To microwave it, bring two cups of water to a boil in your microwave oven. Add one cup of rinsed rice. Cover and microwave at full power for fifteen minutes. Remove from the oven, fluff with a fork, and let stand, covered, for three minutes.

Quinoa (pronounced keen-WAH) is an ancient grain that was used by the Incas and other native South American cultures. It is becoming more popular in American cuisine for a number of reasons. It is the only grain that is a complete protein, containing all of the essential amino acids found in foods like red meat, chicken, or fish. Quinoa cooks very quickly, in about fifteen minutes. It also has a wonderful, celerylike flavor. If you can't find it in your supermarket, try a health-food store. Please note, though: Quinoa is

covered in a bitter residue called saponin that must *always* be rinsed off before cooking; don't skip this important step.

Couscous (pronounced koos-koos) is a staple of North African cuisine. Although it looks like a grain because of its tiny size and irregular shape, couscous is actually a pasta made from semolina flour.

Polenta is a staple food of northern Italy and is becoming increasingly popular in the United States. It is made from coarsely ground cornmeal with a rich flavor and can be found in the rice and grain section of the supermarket (sometimes in the flour section). Prepared polenta is also available in rolls (like cookie dough) in the refrigerated section of some supermarkets and specialty shops. Polenta is often served thick, like mashed potatoes, or allowed to cool and cut into a variety of shapes. It can be reheated before serving by grilling, broiling, or microwaving, and topped with tomato sauce, roasted red pepper sauce, or pesto to make a great side dish.

Bulgur wheat is a nutritious staple of the Middle East. Whole wheat kernels are steamed, dried, and cracked, producing a grain similar in appearance to couscous but with a darker color and chewier texture. Bulgur can be prepared like hot cereal, or used to make dishes like pilafs and tabbouleh salad.

FETA CHEESE POLENTA & PARMESAN CHEESE POLENTA

Time to table: 15 minutes   Serves 2 adults and 2 children

In this recipe, polenta is cooked with chicken broth, a little salt, and sugar. To make a richer-tasting polenta, substitute 1 cup of low-fat milk for 1 cup of the chicken broth. It goes well with Chicken Puttanesca, Lemon Rosemary Roast Chicken, and Chicken With Capers and Sun-Dried Tomatoes.

4 cups low-fat chicken broth or
   water
1 cup Italian polenta or yellow
   cornmeal
½ teaspoon salt
1½ tablespoons sugar

GROWN-UPS
2 tablespoons crumbled feta cheese
Salt and pepper to taste

CHILDREN
2 tablespoons grated Parmesan
   cheese

Combine the chicken broth, polenta, salt, and sugar in a medium saucepan. Bring to a boil over high heat while stirring. Reduce heat to medium and stir until thick, 4–5 minutes or longer, depending on the package instructions.

Transfer half of the polenta into another dish. Fold the feta cheese, salt, and pepper into the adults' portion, and stir the Parmesan cheese into the childrens portion. Serve immediately.

Alternately, you can pour each portion after the cheeses and spices are added into 2 8 × 8-inch baking dishes and allow to cool and set for 20–25 minutes. Cut the polenta into serving-size pieces in any shape you like and reheat it in the microwave for 2–3 minutes. Sprinkle with Parmesan cheese or top with tomato or pesto sauce.

GROWN-UPS
Calories 200; Calories from fat 20
Total fat 2.5 g; Saturated fat 1.5 g
Cholesterol 5 mg; Sodium 580 mg
Carbohydrate 32 g; Dietary fiber 3 g
Sugars 5 g; Protein 12 g

CHILDREN
Calories 200; Calories from fat 20
Total fat 2.5 g; Saturated fat 1.5 g
Cholesterol 5 mg; Sodium 580 mg
Carbohydrate 32 g; Dietary fiber 3 g
Sugars 5 g; Protein 12 g

Pesto Polenta: Fold in 1/4 cup of basil, parsley, or cilantro pesto.

Sun-Dried Tomato Polenta: Fold in 1/4 cup chopped sun-dried tomatoes.

Roasted Red Pepper Polenta: Fold in 1 7¼-ounce jar chopped roasted red peppers.

Corn Polenta: Fold in 1 cup of cut corn.

GREEK CAPELLINI & PARMESAN

CAPELLINI

Time to table: 15 minutes   Serves 2 adults and 2 or 3 children

Capellini is a very thin pasta that cooks in a matter of minutes. Instead of an elaborate sauce, this capellini is tossed with olives, sun-dried tomatoes, and capers. For the children, the pasta is tossed with butter and Parmesan cheese or can be dressed up with olives, tomatoes, or capers, depending on their tastes. To make this into a main course, increase the quantity of pasta to 10–12 ounces and stir in crumbled and browned low-fat Italian sausage. This side dish goes well with Grilled Greek Chicken With Feta Sauce and Veal Cutlets With Fennel Mustard Sauce.

8 ounces capellini
2 tablespoons fresh lemon juice
½ teaspoon garlic powder
Grated Parmesan cheese (for garnish)

GROWN-UPS
8–10 pitted Greek or California olives, coarsely chopped
2 tablespoons oil-packed sun-dried tomatoes, rinsed, drained, and chopped
1 tablespoon capers, drained

1 tablespoon chopped fresh dill or parsley (optional)
Salt and pepper to taste

CHILDREN
½ tablespoon butter, cut into several pieces
2–3 tablespoons grated Parmesan cheese
Sun-dried tomatoes, capers, and olives (optional)
Salt to taste

Bring a large pot of water to a boil. Break the pasta in half before adding to the water, and cook according to package directions. Put 2 tablespoons of the pasta water into a small bowl; add the lemon juice and garlic powder. Drain the pasta and toss with lemon mixture. Transfer half to another dish.

Toss half of the pasta with the olives, sun-dried tomatoes, and capers. Stir in the dill if using. Season with salt and pepper. Cover to keep warm until ready to serve.

Toss the other half of the pasta with butter and Parmesan cheese. Add sun-dried tomatoes and olives, if to the children's liking. Season with salt, if desired.

Garnish with a light sprinkle of Parmesan cheese.

Sausage and Greek Capellini: Remove the casings from 2 or 3 low-fat Italian sausages and brown in a skillet. Add to the pasta and toss until blended.

GROWN-UPS

Calories 240; Calories from fat 30
Total fat 3.50 g; Saturated fat 0 g
Cholesterol 0 mg; Sodium 390 mg
Carbohydrate 41 g; Dietary fiber 3 g
Sugars 4 g; Protein 13 g

CHILDREN

Calories 180; Calories from fat 35
Total fat 4 g; Saturated fat 2 g
Cholesterol 10 mg; Sodium 80 mg
Carbohydrate 26 g; Dietary fiber 0 g
Sugars 1 g; Protein 10 g

ROTINI WITH ROASTED RED PEPPERS
& RAINBOW ROTINI WITH
CHEESE SAUCE

Time to table: 20 minutes   Serves 2 adults and 2 or 3 children

R ainbow rotini is a spiral-shaped pasta that you can buy in three different colors; however, any pasta shape can be used in this recipe. If the children are more fond of one type than another, use the one that they like the best. For the grown-ups, the pasta is tossed with roasted red peppers, fresh basil, and feta cheese. For the children, the pasta is smothered with a more traditional cheese sauce made quickly in the microwave. This recipe goes well with Mediterranean Grilled Halibut, Cajun Spiced Chicken, and Veal Scaloppini.

8 ounces rainbow rotini pasta

GROWN-UPS

1 7¼-ounce jar roasted red peppers, rinsed and chopped
6–8 fresh basil leaves, cut into thin strips
2 tablespoons crumbled feta or grated Parmesan cheese
Salt and pepper to taste

CHILDREN

½ cup low-fat milk
½ tablespoon cornstarch
2 slices American cheese, torn into pieces
Salt to taste

Prepare the pasta according to the package directions. Drain the pasta and transfer half to another dish.

Add the peppers, basil, and feta cheese to half of the pasta, stirring to combine. Season with salt and pepper. Cover to keep warm until ready to serve.

While the pasta is cooking, whisk together the milk and cornstarch in a 4-cup-capacity microwave-safe bowl. Microwave at full power for 60–90 seconds, until the mixture comes to a boil. Whisk the mixture again and microwave at full power for 1 more minute. Add the cheese and stir until melted. Season with salt, if desired. Pour over the pasta for the children.

Rotini With Sun-Dried Tomatoes: Substitute 1/4 cup sun-dried tomatoes for the red peppers.

GROWN-UPS
Calories 270; Calories from fat 30
Total fat 3.5 g; Saturated fat 1.5 g
Cholesterol 10 mg; Sodium 480 mg
Carbohydrate 48 g; Dietary fiber 2 g
Sugars 5 g; Protein 10 g

CHILDREN
Calories 220; Calories from fat 50
Total fat 6 g; Saturated fat 3.5 g
Cholesterol 15 mg; Sodium 220 mg
Carbohydrate 32 g; Dietary fiber 1 g
Sugars 3 g; Protein 9 g

SAFFRON GARLIC ORZO RISOTTO
··

& ORZO RISOTTO WITH CHEESE
··

Time to table: 15 minutes   Serves 2 adults and 2 or 3 children

Orzo, tiny rice-shaped pasta, is prepared like risotto. Shallots and garlic are sautéed in a small amount of olive oil, then the orzo is cooked in added chicken broth. The pasta comes out thick and creamy. The adults' variation is flavored with lemon, saffron, fresh parsley, and pimientos. The color contrast between the bright yellow saffron orzo and the dazzling red pimientos is striking. This goes well with Shrimp Piccata, Chicken Puttanesca, and Moroccan Spiced Lamb.

> **❝***This was really pretty. My son really likes the children's version. I've made it several times at his request.***❞**

1 teaspoon olive oil
1 shallot, finely diced, about ¼ cup
3–4 garlic cloves, minced
2 14½-ounce cans low-sodium
    chicken broth
1½ cups orzo
¼ cup grated Parmesan cheese
Grated Parmesan cheese to taste

GROWN-UPS
1–2 pinches ground saffron, about
    ¹⁄₃₂ of a teaspoon, see note

1–2 tablespoons fresh lemon juice
2 tablespoons chopped fresh parsley
1–2 tablespoons chopped pimientos
    (optional)
Salt and pepper to taste

CHILDREN
½ tablespoon butter, cut into
    several pieces
¼ cup grated mozzarella cheese
Salt to taste

Heat the olive oil in a nonstick saucepan over medium-high heat. Add the shallot and cook until soft, about 2 minutes. Add the garlic and cook for 1 minute, until fragrant. Add the chicken broth and bring to a boil. Add the orzo and cook until tender, according to the package directions. Drain and toss with Parmesan cheese. Transfer half to another dish.

Stir the saffron and the lemon juice into half of the orzo. The orzo should be a bright yellow color. Stir in the parsley and pimientos, if using. Season with salt and pepper. Sprinkle with more Parmesan cheese.

Add the butter and mozzarella cheese to the children's servings and stir until melted. Season with salt, if desired. Top with a light sprinkle of Parmesan cheese.

Note: If using saffron threads, grind them with a mortar and pestle or break them into small pieces and soak in lemon juice.

GROWN-UPS
Calories 220; Calories from fat 25
Total fat 2.5 g; Saturated fat 1.5 g
Cholesterol 5 mg; Sodium 240 mg
Carbohydrate 37 g; Dietary fiber 2 g
Sugars 3 g; Protein 11 g

CHILDREN
Calories 190; Calories from fat 50
Total fat 6 g; Saturated fat 3 g
Cholesterol 15 mg; Sodium 180 mg
Carbohydrate 24 g; Dietary fiber 1 g
Sugars 2 g; Protein 10 g

LEMON-HERB ORZO WITH FETA CHEESE & LEMON ORZO WITH PARMESAN CHEESE

Time to table: 20 minutes   **Serves 2 adults and 2 or 3 children**

In this recipe orzo is seasoned with a combination of savory herbs and tart feta cheese. For the children, the orzo is simply seasoned with butter and Parmesan cheese. This recipe goes well with Chili Baked Salmon, Grilled Greek Chicken With Feta Sauce, and Veal Scaloppini.

❝*I really like feta cheese but my husband does not. Instead of tossing the adults' portion with the cheese, I left it out and put Parmesan and feta cheese on the table. We both helped ourselves.*❞

1½ cups orzo

GROWN-UPS
1–2 tablespoons fresh lemon juice
2 tablespoons chopped fresh parsley
1 teaspoon chopped fresh thyme or
   ½ teaspoon dried thyme soaked
   in lemon juice
1 green onion, chopped fine
2 tablespoons crumbled feta or goat
   cheese, reduced-fat or regular

Salt and freshly ground black
   pepper to taste

CHILDREN
½ tablespoon butter
1 teaspoon lemon zest
2 tablespoons Parmesan cheese
Salt to taste

Cook the orzo according to the package directions. Drain and transfer half to each of two dishes.

Stir the lemon juice, parsley, thyme, and green onion into half of the pasta. Fold in the feta cheese. Season with salt and pepper.

Toss the pasta for the children with butter, lemon zest, and Parmesan cheese. Season with salt, if desired.

Note: You can purchase herbed feta cheese and substitute it for the plain in this recipe, but adjust the quantity of herbs added to taste.

GROWN-UPS
Calories 190; Calories from fat 25
Total fat 3 g; Saturated fat 1.5 g
Cholesterol 10 mg; Sodium 110 mg
Carbohydrate 34 g; Dietary fiber 1 g
Sugars 2 g; Protein 7 g

CHILDREN
Calories 140; Calories from fat 35
Total fat 3.5 g; Saturated fat 2 g
Cholesterol 10 mg; Sodium 80 mg
Carbohydrate 22 g; Dietary fiber 1 g
Sugars 1 g; Protein 5 g

LIME CILANTRO PILAF & TOASTED
••
ALMOND RICE PILAF
•••••••••••••••••••••••••••••••••••••

Time to table: 30 minutes   Serves 2 adults and 2 or 3 children

Toasted almonds accentuate the nutty, sweet taste of basmati rice. For the grown-ups, the rice is flavored with fresh lime juice and cilantro. One way to make rice more visually appealing to children is to use large cookie cutters as rice molds. Place a cookie cutter on the plate and fill with rice, packing it in. Gently remove the mold before serving. This goes well with Grilled Shrimp With Thai Dipping Sauce, Indonesian Chicken Satay, and Pork Chops With Spicy Apple Chutney.

❝It was wonderful. The lime and cilantro are so good together. The children liked the rice, but two of them picked out the almonds. Next time, I'll add the almonds only to the adults' variation.❞

1 teaspoon olive oil
1 medium shallot, chopped
2 cups water
½ teaspoon salt
1 cup basmati rice or white rice
3 tablespoons toasted slivered almonds

GROWN-UPS
2 tablespoons fresh lime juice
1–2 green onions, chopped fine
¼ cup minced cilantro
½ tablespoon butter (optional)
Salt and pepper to taste

CHILDREN
½ tablespoon butter
Salt to taste

Heat the olive oil in a saucepan over medium-high heat for 2 minutes. Add the shallots and stir until soft, 2–3 minutes. Add the water and salt; bring to boil. Add the rice, cover, reduce heat, and simmer for 15–20 minutes. Stir and let stand, covered, for 3 minutes. Stir in the almonds. Transfer half to another dish.

Stir in the lime juice, green onions, and cilantro to half of the rice. Add the butter, if using, and stir until melted. Season with salt and pepper.

Add the butter to the remaining rice and stir until melted. Season with salt, if desired.

GROWN-UPS
Calories 240; Calories from fat 40
Total fat 4.5 g; Saturated fat .05 g
Cholesterol 0 mg; Sodium 580 mg
Carbohydrate 45 g; Dietary fiber 1 g
Sugars 1 g; Protein 5 g

CHILDREN
Calories 180; Calories from fat 50
Total fat 5 g; Saturated fat 1.5 g
Cholesterol 5 mg; Sodium 200 mg
Carbohydrate 29 g; Dietary fiber 1 g
Sugars 1 g; Protein 4 g

Note: Almonds can be toasted in the microwave oven, on top of the stove, or in a conventional oven. Microwave for 6–8 minutes, stirring every 2 minutes; toast in a small skillet over medium-high heat for about 5 minutes, shaking the pan frequently; or roast at 350 degrees F. for 10–15 minutes, stirring occasionally.

SESAME ORIENTAL RICE
& SESAME STEAMED RICE

Time to table: 25 minutes   **Serves 2 adults and 2 children**

Oriental seasonings heighten the aromatic qualities of basmati rice. Toasted sesame seeds add crunch, while dark sesame oil and teriyaki sauce add flavor. This recipe goes well with Lime Skewered Shrimp, Teriyaki Honey Glazed Drumsticks, Shanghai Chicken Kabobs, and Hoisin Glazed Chicken.

❝*This was great with stir-fry chicken.*❞

1 cup basmati rice or white rice

GROWN-UPS
1 tablespoon toasted sesame seeds
1 tablespoon teriyaki sauce
1 tablespoon lemon juice
1 teaspoon dark sesame oil
1 green onion, chopped
Salt to taste

CHILDREN
1 tablespoon toasted sesame seeds
  (optional)
1 teaspoon sesame oil (optional)
1 tablespoon teriyaki sauce
  (optional)

Cook the rice according to the package instructions. Divide into two dishes.

Stir the sesame seeds, teriyaki sauce, lemon juice, sesame oil, and green onions into the adults' portion. Season to taste with salt.

If desired stir the sesame seeds, sesame oil, and teriyaki sauce into the children's servings.

GROWN-UPS
Calories 250; Calories from fat 25
Total fat 3 g; Saturated fat 0.5 g
Cholesterol 0 mg; Sodium 350 mg
Carbohydrate 43 g; Dietary fiber 1 g
Sugars 1 g; Protein 5 g

CHILDREN
Calories 150; Calories from fat 30
Total fat 3 g; Saturated fat 0.5 g
Cholesterol 0 mg; Sodium 190 mg
Carbohydrate 28 g; Dietary fiber 1 g
Sugars 0 g; Protein 3 g

GREEN CHILE RICE & CHEDDAR

CHEESE RICE

Time to table: 25 minutes   Serves 2 adults and 2 or 3 children

Green chiles and tomatoes come together to create a tantalizing southwestern-style side dish. In the mildly flavored version for the children, the chiles are replaced with grated Cheddar cheese, which melts as it is stirred into the hot rice. This goes well with Southwestern Red Snapper, Bayou Baked Fish, and Chicken With Spicy Mole Sauce.

1 14½-ounce can stewed tomatoes
    or peeled, diced tomatoes in
    juice
½ cup water
1 cup white rice

GROWN-UPS
1 teaspoon chili powder
¼ teaspoon cumin

1 4-ounce can chopped green
    chiles, mild, medium, or hot
1–2 green onions, sliced thin
Salt and pepper to taste

CHILDREN
¼ cup grated Cheddar cheese or
    Monterey Jack cheese
Salt to taste

Pour the stewed tomatoes and water into a saucepan. Mash the tomatoes with a potato masher to eliminate any large chunks. Bring to a boil and stir in the rice. Reduce heat to low, cover, and simmer until the water is absorbed and the rice is tender. Refer to the package instructions for exact times. Remove from heat. Fluff with a fork, cover, and let stand for 3 minutes. Divide evenly into two bowls.

To half of the rice, stir in the chili powder, cumin, green chiles, and green onions. Season with salt and pepper.

Stir the cheese into the children's servings until partially melted. Season with salt, if desired.

GROWN-UPS
Calories 230; Calories from fat 5
Total fat 1 g; Saturated fat 0 g
Cholesterol 0 mg; Sodium 470 mg
Carbohydrate 49 g; Dietary fiber 4 g
Sugars 7 g; Protein 5 g

CHILDREN
Calories 180; Calories from fat 30
Total fat 3.5 g; Saturated fat 2 g
Cholesterol 10 mg; Sodium 210 mg
Carbohydrate 30 g; Dietary fiber 1 g
Sugars 5 g; Protein 5 g

WILD MUSHROOM HERBED QUINOA
···
& NUTTY QUINOA
·······································

Time to table: 20 minutes   Serves 2 adults and 2 or 3 children

Dried porcini mushrooms and quinoa are paired in this smoky, woodsy tasting side dish. For the children, mild quinoa is accented with almonds and butter. Unlike rice and other grains, quinoa almost never absorbs all the cooking liquid. Drain in a fine mesh strainer after cooking. This recipe goes well with Green Peppercorn Steak, Lemon Rosemary Roast Chicken, and Veal Scaloppini.

❝*This was new to me—both the porcini mushrooms and the quinoa. The combination was wonderful. I'm a mushroom lover, but my children and husband are not. I added the mushrooms to my serving, which I thoroughly enjoyed.*❞

1 cup quinoa
1 14½-ounce can low-sodium
  chicken broth and water to
  measure 2 cups

GROWN-UPS
½ ounce dried porcini mushrooms
2 tablespoons chopped fresh flat-
  leaf parsley

1 green onion, chopped fine
Salt and pepper to taste

CHILDREN
½ tablespoon butter
2 tablespoons slivered almonds or
  pine nuts (optional)
Salt to taste

Put the quinoa in a wire mesh strainer and rinse thoroughly under cold water. Transfer to a medium-size saucepan. Pour the chicken stock and water into the saucepan. Bring to a boil, cover, reduce heat, and simmer for 15 minutes. Drain away excess liquid. Divide equally into two dishes.

While the quinoa is cooking, place the mushrooms in a 1-cup microwave-safe bowl. Pour in enough water to just cover the mushrooms. Cover with a lid or plastic wrap and microwave at full power for

1 minute. Reduce setting to "low" or "simmer" and microwave for 8 minutes. The mushrooms should be very soft and pliable. Remove the mushrooms from the liquid and rinse under cold water to remove any sand. Chop the mushrooms into small pieces. (Save the mushroom liquid to add to soups or gravy. Strain it through a coffee filter and freeze for later use.)

Stir the mushrooms, parsley, and green onions into half of the quinoa. Season with salt and pepper.

Add the butter and almonds (if using) to the children's portion. Stir until the butter is melted. Season with salt if desired.

GROWN-UPS
Calories 200; Calories from fat 25
Total fat 3 g; Saturated fat 0 g
Cholesterol 0 mg; Sodium 380 mg
Carbohydrate 33 g; Dietary fiber 4 g
Sugars 0 g; Protein 11 g

CHILDREN
Calories 170; Calories from fat 60
Total fat 6 g; Saturated fat 1.5 g
Cholesterol 5 mg; Sodium 60 mg
Carbohydrate 21 g; Dietary fiber 2 g
Sugars 0 g; Protein 7 g

CILANTRO QUINOA PILAF
....

& FRUITED QUINOA PILAF
....

Time to table: 20 minutes   Serves 2 adults and 2 or 3 children

In this recipe, quinoa is combined with golden raisins and dried apricots; savory toasted pine nuts boost the flavor and add crunch. Omit the nuts from the children's portion if they're not to the kids' liking. For the grown-ups, fresh cilantro and a splash of lemon juice finish the dish. This recipe goes well with Orange Curry Chicken, Chicken With Spicy Mole Sauce, and Bayou Baked Fish.

1 14½-ounce can low-sodium
   chicken broth and water to
   measure 2 cups
4 Mediterranean-style dried
   apricots, diced fine
2 tablespoons golden raisins
1 cup quinoa, well rinsed and
   drained
¼ cup toasted pine nuts or toasted
   slivered almonds

GROWN-UPS
½ cup finely chopped cilantro
1 teaspoon grated lemon zest
1 tablespoon lemon juice
Salt and pepper to taste

CHILDREN
½ tablespoon butter
Salt to taste

Pour the chicken broth and water into a medium-size saucepan. Add the apricots, raisins, and quinoa. Bring to a boil, reduce heat, cover, and simmer for 15 minutes. Pour into a strainer and drain away excess liquid. Stir in the pine nuts (optional), then separate into adult- and child-size servings.

Stir the cilantro, lemon zest, and lemon juice into the adult servings; season with salt and pepper.

Stir the butter into the children's servings until melted. Season with salt if desired.

GROWN-UPS
Calories 270; Calories from fat 60
Total fat 7 g; Saturated fat 1 g
Cholesterol 0 mg; Sodium 90 mg
Carbohydrate 42 g; Dietary fiber 4 g
Sugars 9 g; Protein 11 g

CHILDREN
Calories 190; Calories from fat 60
Total fat 7 g; Saturated fat 2 g
Cholesterol 5 mg; Sodium 75 mg
Carbohydrate 27 g; Dietary fiber 2 g
Sugars 6 g; Protein 7 g

LEMON PARSLEY COUSCOUS
& LEMON MINT COUSCOUS

Time to table: 10 minutes   Serves 2 adults and 2 or 3 children

In this recipe, water, lemon juice, and sugar are used to make an almost lemonadelike broth. For the grown-ups, green onions and fresh parsley are combined to finish this slightly tart and savory side dish. For the children, the flavors are mellowed with butter and mint. This recipe goes well with Chili Baked Salmon, Cajun Spiced Chicken, and Chicken in Chipotle Chile Barbecue Sauce.

½ teaspoon grated lemon zest
  or ¼ teaspoon dried
3 tablespoons fresh lemon juice
1 tablespoon sugar
¼ teaspoon salt
1¼ cups water
1 cup couscous

GROWN-UPS
1–2 green onions, minced

2 tablespoons minced flat-leaf
  parsley
Salt and pepper to taste

CHILDREN
½ tablespoon butter
1 tablespoon dried mint or 2
  tablespoons fresh
Salt to taste

Add the lemon zest, lemon juice, sugar, salt, and water to a 1–2-quart-size microwave-safe dish. Microwave at full power for 3–4 minutes, until the mixture begins to boil. Stir in the couscous, cover, and let stand for 5 minutes. Fluff with a fork. Transfer half to another dish.

Stir the green onions and parsley into half of the couscous. Season with salt and pepper.

Stir the butter into the children's servings until melted; fold in the mint. Season with salt if desired.

Note: Couscous can be made on the stovetop as well. Just bring the liquid to a boil, add the couscous, and cover; remove from the heat, and let stand for 5 minutes.

GROWN-UPS
Calories 180; Calories from fat 0
Total fat 0 g; Saturated fat 0 g
Cholesterol 0 mg; Sodium 150 mg
Carbohydrate 38 g; Dietary fiber 3 g
Sugars 5 g; Protein 6 g

CHILDREN
Calories 140; Calories from fat 20
Total fat 2 g; Saturated fat 1 g
Cholesterol 5 mg; Sodium 100 mg
Carbohydrate 25 g; Dietary fiber 2 g
Sugars 3 g; Protein 4 g

MIDDLE EASTERN CRACKED-WHEAT PILAF & CRACKED-WHEAT PILAF WITH APPLES AND RAISINS

Time to table: 20 minutes   Serves 2 adults and 2 or 3 children

Bulgur wheat makes an excellent pilaf. For the grown-ups, this chewy, high-fiber grain is paired with chickpeas (garbanzo beans) and olives, also staples of Middle Eastern cuisine. Seasoned with lemon juice, garlic, and hot pepper sauce, this healthy side dish is ready in short order. For the children, dried apples, raisins, and nuts make their variation almost like dessert. This recipe goes well with Moroccan Spiced Lamb, Curried Steak With Orange Sauce, and Orange Curry Chicken.

1 cup bulgur wheat

GROWN-UPS

1 teaspoon grated lemon zest or ½ teaspoon dried

3 tablespoons lemon juice

1–2 green onions, sliced fine

1 small garlic clove, pressed

½ teaspoon Tabasco or hot pepper sauce

1 8¾-ounce can garbanzo beans, drained and coarsely chopped

Half of a 2¼-ounce can sliced black olives

Salt and cayenne pepper to taste

CHILDREN

¼ cup chopped dried apples (see note)

2 tablespoons raisins or currants (see note)

¼ cup or more apple juice or water (see note)

2 tablespoons chopped toasted pecans, walnuts, or almonds (optional)

½ tablespoon butter

Salt to taste

Bring 2 quarts of water to a boil. Add the bulgur wheat, reduce heat to medium, and cook, uncovered, for 15 minutes. Pour into a strainer and drain well. Transfer half to another dish for the children.

Stir in the apples, raisins, pecans (if using), and butter. Season with salt, if desired.

Put the lemon zest, lemon juice, green onions, garlic, Tabasco sauce, garbanzo beans, and olives in a small microwave-safe dish. Microwave at full power for 2–3 minutes. Fold into the bulgur wheat for the grown-ups. Season with salt and cayenne.

Note: If desired, the apples and raisins can be softened and plumped in apple juice. Place the dried fruits in a microwave-safe dish and cover with apple juice. Microwave at full power for 1 minute. Let stand, then drain when ready to use.

GROWN-UPS
Calories 240; Calories from fat 30
Total fat 3.5 g; Saturated fat 0 g
Cholesterol 0 mg; Sodium 330 mg
Carbohydrate 48 g; Dietary fiber 13 g
Sugars 2 g; Protein 9 g

CHILDREN
Calories 170; Calories from fat 50
Total fat 6 g; Saturated fat 1.5 g
Cholesterol 5 mg; Sodium 50 mg
Carbohydrate 29 g; Dietary fiber 6 g
Sugars 10 g; Protein 4 g

VEGETABLES

· ·

Many parents will agree that getting children to eat vegetables is not always easy. My own informal survey revealed that most children have a few favorites. My testers admitted that they were surprised when their children ate vegetables that they had never tried before. The roasted vegetables, in particular, are appealing because roasting caramelizes the natural sugars, imparting a slightly sweet taste.

Sometimes children prefer a particular vegetable either frozen or canned over fresh. In my own childhood I disliked boiled potatoes but I loved canned new potatoes. If your children will not eat a particular vegetable fresh, try another form. And don't worry about the nutrition value: According to a recent study at the University of Illinois, canned and frozen fruits and vegetables can contain *more* vitamins than fresh. Produce that is canned or frozen is often processed right after picking, locking in the available nutrients, while fresh produce loses nutrients after picking, shipping, and during sometimes lengthy storage.

If your children tolerate food on their plates that they do not normally eat, try giving them a spoonful of the adults' variation. This can help them begin to develop an appreciation for new foods and flavors.

ASPARAGUS WITH DILL HOLLANDAISE SAUCE & ASPARAGUS WITH CREAMY CHEESE SAUCE

Time to table: 15 minutes   **Serves 2 adults and 2 to 4 children**

Often referred to as the aristocrat of vegetables, asparagus was cultivated and prized by the ancient Greeks and Romans. Asparagus with hollandaise sauce is a classic pairing. Traditional hollandaise is made almost exclusively with egg yolks and butter. To whittle away the calories and fat, low-fat milk is used here as the base. A pinch of ground saffron gives the sauce the distinctive yellow color of hollandaise. Fresh dill and lemon juice complete the adults' version. The children's variation is transformed into a creamy cheese sauce. This recipe is great with Dill Crab Cakes, Bayou Baked Fish, and Lemon Rosemary Roast Chicken.

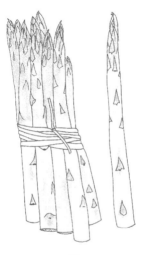

❝I haven't prepared hollandaise sauce in years because it's so rich. This tasted so wonderful, and I could eat it without feeling guilty. I especially liked the dill.❞

1¼–1½ pounds fresh asparagus,
about 20–25 spears, rinsed and
trimmed, or 3–4 cups frozen

DILL HOLLANDAISE SAUCE

1 cup 1 percent milk
1 tablespoon cornstarch
½ teaspoon dry mustard
Dash of saffron or turmeric for
color
1 tablespoon unsalted butter

GROWN-UPS
1–2 tablespoons fresh dill or flat-
leaf parsley, chopped fine, or
1 tablespoon dried

2 tablespoons fresh lemon juice
Salt and pepper to taste

CHILDREN
2 slices American cheese or
Cheddar cheese cut into small
pieces
Salt to taste

Leave the asparagus whole or cut into 2-inch pieces. Bring a large pot of water to a boil. Add the asparagus. Bring back to a boil and cook for 2–3 minutes until crisp tender. Drain and cover to keep warm until ready to serve. (Alternatively, cook the asparagus in the microwave. Place the asparagus in a large baking dish with the buds pointing to the center. Add a few tablespoons of water. Cover with vented plastic wrap. Microwave at full power for 4 minutes. Rotate the dish, and microwave for another 3 minutes. The asparagus should be tender. If not, microwave for another 2–3 minutes.) If using frozen asparagus, follow package directions for heating.

Whisk together the milk, cornstarch, dry mustard, and saffron in a large microwave-safe bowl (at least 4-cup capacity, since the mixture expands considerably as it heats). Microwave at full power for 2 minutes or more, until the mixture begins to boil. Remove from the microwave and whisk several times. Return to the microwave and cook at full power for 1 minute longer. Whisk in the butter until melted. (The sauce can be made on the stovetop, too. Just bring the mixture to a boil over moderately high heat and cook for 1 minute after it begins to boil.)

Transfer half of the sauce to another dish. Stir in the dill and lemon juice. Season with salt and pepper. Add the cheese to the remaining sauce. Microwave for an additional 30–45 seconds until the cheese is melted. Stir to blend. Season with salt, if desired.

Serve the asparagus topped with a few tablespoons of either sauce.

GROWN-UPS	CHILDREN
Calories 110; Calories from fat 40	Calories 80; Calories from fat 45
Total fat 4.5 g; Saturated fat 2.5 g	Total fat 5 g; Saturated fat 3 g
Cholesterol 10 mg; Sodium 35 mg	Cholesterol 15 mg; Sodium 170 mg
Carbohydrate 14 g; Dietary fiber 4 g	Carbohydrate 6 g; Dietary fiber 1 g
Sugars 6 g; Protein 6 g	Sugars 3 g; Protein 5 g

Cauliflower With Dill Hollandaise Sauce: Substitute cooked cauliflower for the asparagus.

Broccoli With Dill Hollandaise Sauce: Substitute cooked broccoli for the asparagus.

DILLY GREEN BEANS
& NUTTY GREEN BEANS

Time to table: 20 minutes   Serves 2 adults and 2 or 3 children

In this recipe, green beans are seasoned with fresh dill, chopped toasted walnuts, a full-flavored walnut oil, and a splash of fresh lemon juice. The combination is rich and earthy. A good-quality walnut oil will have a strong aroma when the bottle is opened. If the nuts are roasted first, the oil will be that much more intensely flavored. For the children, the green beans are simply seasoned with butter and lemon zest. This side dish works well with Grilled Greek Chicken With Feta Sauce, Veal Cutlets With Fennel Mustard Sauce, and Chicken Puttanesca.

❝We really liked the combination of flavors. I went
to a specialty store to get the walnut oil, and it was
worth it. The flavor is so pronounced that only
a small amount is needed.❞

1¼ pounds green beans, rinsed and
trimmed, or 3–4 cups frozen

1–2 tablespoons chopped toasted
walnuts (optional)

GROWN-UPS
½ tablespoon walnut or hazelnut oil
1 green onion, chopped fine
½ teaspoon grated lemon zest
1 tablespoon fresh lemon juice
1–2 tablespoons chopped fresh dill
Salt and pepper to taste

CHILDREN
½ tablespoon butter, cut into small
pieces
½ teaspoon grated lemon zest
Salt to taste
1 tablespoon chopped toasted
walnuts (optional)

Leave the beans whole or cut into 2-inch pieces. Bring a large pot of
water to a boil. Add the beans; bring back to a boil and cook uncovered for 2–3 minutes until crisp tender. Drain and cover to keep warm
until ready to serve. If using frozen green beans, follow the package
instructions for heating.

Blend together the walnut oil, green onion, lemon zest, lemon juice,
and fresh dill in a serving bowl. Add half of the green beans, tossing to
combine. Season with salt and pepper. Garnish with chopped walnuts,
if desired.

Add the butter and lemon zest to the remaining green beans. Toss
until the butter is melted. Season with salt and garnish with chopped
walnuts, if desired.

Note: Zest is the perfumy outermost layer of the lemon. Only the colored portion of the skin is considered the zest (not the white part).
Gently grate a lemon (after scrubbing) over the fine gauge of a
flat grater. Do this directly over the food to be seasoned or over a
plate or bowl to capture the zest as it falls. The aromatic oils of the
skin are what add so much flavor without the bitterness of the inner
rind. A medium-size lemon will yield 2–3 teaspoons of zest.

GROWN-UPS	CHILDREN
Calories 70; Calories from fat 30	Calories 40; Calories from fat 20
Total fat 3.5 g; Saturated fat 0 g	Total fat 2 g; Saturated fat 1 g
Cholesterol 0 mg; Sodium 10 mg	Cholesterol 5 mg; Sodium 0 mg
Carbohydrate 9 g; Dietary fiber 4 g	Carbohydrate 5 g; Dietary fiber 3 g
Sugars 3 g; Protein 2 g	Sugars 2 g; Protein 1 g

Dilly Snap Peas: Substitute snap peas for the green beans.
Dilly Green Peas: Substitute green peas for the green beans.

GREEK-STYLE GREEN BEANS
& BUTTERY GREEN BEANS

Time to table: 15–20 minutes   **Serves 2 adults and 2 or 3 children**

Colorful, sweet, and savory, these green beans are a snap to prepare. Crisp-tender green beans are tossed with a Mediterranean-inspired blend of sun-dried tomatoes and Greek olives. For the children, the beans are seasoned with butter and lemon. This recipe goes well with Mediterranean Grilled Halibut, Lemon Rosemary Roast Chicken, and Veal Scaloppini.

1¼ pounds fresh green beans, rinsed and trimmed, or 3–4 cups frozen

1 tablespoon tomato paste
1–2 tablespoons water
Salt and pepper to taste

GROWN-UPS
¼ cup oil-packed sun-dried tomatoes, well rinsed, drained, and chopped fine
1 small garlic clove, minced
4–5 Greek or California olives, chopped

CHILDREN
½ tablespoon butter, cut into small pieces
½ teaspoon grated lemon zest
Salt to taste

❝Easy and quick. I usually serve all our vegetables plain, the way my kids prefer them. It was a nice change for my husband and me to have something different, but not too complicated either.❞

Leave the beans whole or cut into 2-inch pieces. Bring a large pot of water to a boil. Add the beans; bring back to a boil, and cook for 2–3 minutes until crisp tender. Drain and cover to keep warm until ready to serve. If using frozen green beans, follow the package instructions for heating.

Combine the tomatoes, garlic, olives, tomato paste, and water in a serving bowl. Add half of the green beans, tossing to combine. Season with salt and pepper. Add the butter and lemon zest to the remaining green beans. Toss until the butter is melted. Season with salt, if desired.

Note: Tomato paste can be purchased in tubes. Use only the amount necessary and refrigerate the rest. If using canned tomato paste, freeze the leftovers for later use.

GROWN-UPS
Calories 70; Calories from fat 10
Total fat 1.5 g; Saturated fat 0 g
Cholesterol 0 mg; Sodium 230 mg
Carbohydrate 14 g; Dietary fiber 5 g
Sugars 6 g; Protein 3 g

CHILDREN
Calories 40; Calories from fat 20
Total fat 2 g; Saturated fat 1 g
Cholesterol 5 mg; Sodium 0 mg
Carbohydrate 5 g; Dietary fiber 3 g
Sugars 2 g; Protein 1 g

Greek-Style Butter Beans: Substitute yellow wax beans for the green beans.

Greek-Style Snap Peas: Substitute snap peas for the green beans.

GARLIC ROASTED BROCCOLI
··
& SIMPLY ROASTED BROCCOLI
··

Time to table: 25 minutes   Serves 2 adults and 2 or 3 children

Roasting at high temperatures caramelizes vegetables' natural sugars and makes broccoli crunchy and slightly sweet. As the broccoli roasts, much of the moisture evaporates. Although the calories and fiber are still the same, the yield is smaller. To compensate, prepare a little more than usual, perhaps as much as two bunches. This recipe goes well with Chili Baked Salmon, Shrimp Piccata, and Pork With Burgundy Cranberry Sauce.

**❝We liked this a lot and will make it again.
Cauliflower was great this way, too. In fact,
I mixed them together.❞**

1½–2 bunches fresh broccoli   ¼ *teaspoon pepper*
Olive oil cooking spray   ¼ *teaspoon garlic powder*
¼ *teaspoon salt*   ¼ *teaspoon onion powder*

Preheat oven to 450 degrees F. Wash the broccoli and cut into even florets. The stems can be roasted too. Just peel and cut into bite-size pieces.

Coat a large baking sheet with cooking spray. Place the broccoli pieces in a single layer. Lightly spray with cooking spray. Season half with salt, pepper, garlic powder, and onion powder. Sprinkle the other half with seasonings that the children enjoy. Place the baking sheet on the center rack of the oven and bake for 18–22 minutes. The broccoli should be browned and tender.

GROWN-UPS
Calories 45; Calories from fat 5
Total fat 0.5 g; Saturated fat 0 g
Cholesterol 0 mg; Sodium 120 mg
Carbohydrate 8 g; Dietary fiber 4 g
Sugars 3 g; Protein 4 g

CHILDREN
Calories 35; Calories from fat 0
Total fat 0 g; Saturated fat 0 g
Cholesterol 0 mg; Sodium 80 mg
Carbohydrate 6 g; Dietary fiber 4 g
Sugars 2 g; Protein 3 g

Roasted Cauliflower: Substitute cauliflower for the broccoli.

Roasted Asparagus: Substitute asparagus for the broccoli. Peel the skin from very thick or woody asparagus. Roast for only about 10 minutes.

TERIYAKI SESAME BROCCOLI
& HONEY SESAME BROCCOLI

Time to table: 15 minutes   Serves 2 adults and 2 or 3 children

In this recipe, cooked broccoli is tossed with honey and lemon juice. For the grown-ups, the broccoli is further accented with teriyaki sauce and sesame seeds. For the children, it's seasoned with salt and melted butter. This recipe goes well with Hoisin Glazed Chicken, Lime Skewered Shrimp, and Shanghai Chicken Kabobs.

1 bunch broccoli, rinsed and separated into florets
1 tablespoon honey
1–2 tablespoons lemon juice or orange juice
Toasted sesame seeds for garnish

GROWN-UPS
1 tablespoon teriyaki marinade
Salt and pepper to taste

CHILDREN
½ tablespoon butter, cut into small pieces
Salt to taste

*"My children like both broccoli and teriyaki. I just
make the adult variation for the whole family."*

Bring a large pot of water to a boil. Add the broccoli, bring back to
a boil, and cook for 3–4 minutes until crisp tender. Drain. In a small
bowl, mix the honey and lemon juice together. Pour over the broccoli
and gently toss to combine. Transfer half to another dish.

Stir the teriyaki marinade into half of the broccoli. Season with salt
and pepper; garnish with toasted sesame seeds.

Add the butter to the remaining broccoli and toss until melted.
Season with salt and garnish with toasted sesame seeds, if desired.

GROWN-UPS
Calories 60; Calories from fat 0
Total fat 0 g; Saturated fat 0 g
Cholesterol 0 mg; Sodium 380 mg
Carbohydrate 13 g; Dietary fiber 4 g
Sugars 8 g; Protein 5 g

CHILDREN
Calories 50; Calories from fat 20
Total fat 2 g; Saturated fat 1 g
Cholesterol 5 mg; Sodium 25 mg
Carbohydrate 8 g; Dietary fiber 3 g
Sugars 5 g; Protein 3 g

Teriyaki Sesame Asparagus: Substitute asparagus for the broccoli.

Note: To toast sesame seeds, heat a nonstick skillet over medium-high
heat for 2 minutes. Add the sesame seeds and shake pan frequently
for about 3–5 minutes until the seeds become light brown in color.

CILANTRO PESTO CORN ON THE COB
& BUTTERY CORN ON THE COB

Time to table: 10–15 minutes   Serves 2 adults and 2 to 4 children

This light cilantro pesto is delicious with corn. Parsley may be sub-
stituted for the cilantro, if desired. This recipe goes well with
Grilled Lamb Chops With Thai Mint Sauce, Chicken in Chipotle
Chile Barbecue Sauce, and Cajun Spiced Chicken.

❝My husband does not like cilantro, so I made the pesto with parsley, which we both enjoy. I never have trouble getting our children to eat corn on the cob. It's a favorite.❞

4–6 ears of fresh corn, husked and
   desilked

GROWN-UPS
Cilantro Pesto (recipe follows)
Salt and pepper to taste

CHILDREN
½ tablespoon butter
Salt to taste

In a large pot, bring to a boil enough water to cover the corn. *Do not add salt.* Add the corn, bring back to a boil, and cook for 3–5 minutes, until the corn is tender. Remove the corn with tongs. For young children, rinse the corn under cold water for a few seconds to cool it down before serving.

Spread a small amount of butter on the children's corn, or let them do this themselves using a butter knife or plastic knife. Season with salt, if desired.

Let the grown-ups help themselves to the Cilantro Pesto and salt and pepper.

CILANTRO PESTO

1 bunch fresh cilantro or flat-leaf
   parsley, stems removed
1 clove garlic, peeled
1 tablespoon fresh lime (if using
   cilantro) or lemon (if using
   parsley) juice

1 tablespoon rice vinegar
¼ teaspoon salt

Add the cilantro, garlic, lime juice, rice vinegar, and salt to the bowl of a food processor. Process until chopped. Transfer to a small bowl and place on the table.

GROWN-UPS
Calories 90; Calories from fat 10
Total fat 1 g; Saturated fat 0 g
Cholesterol 0 mg; Sodium 310 mg
Carbohydrate 21 g; Dietary fiber 3 g
Sugars 2 g; Protein 3 g

CHILDREN
Calories 120; Calories from fat 45
Total fat 5 g; Saturated fat 2.5 g
Cholesterol 10 mg; Sodium 15 mg
Carbohydrate 19 g; Dietary fiber 2 g
Sugars 2 g; Protein 3 g

Cilantro Pesto Cut Corn: Use 3–4 cups of canned, frozen, or fresh cut corn. After cooking, stir the cilantro pesto into the corn for the grown-ups. Stir the butter into the corn for the children.

PARSLEY CREAMED CORN
& SWEET CREAMED CORN

Time to table: 25 minutes   Serves 2 adults and 2 or 3 children

Fresh-cut creamed corn is delightfully sweet. For the grown-ups, parsley and green onions add a nice color contrast and more flavor. Butter is more in line with the children's tastes. This recipe goes well with Green Peppercorn Steak, Lemon Rosemary Roast Chicken, and Bayou Baked Fish.

4–6 ears of fresh corn, husked and desilked
2 cups water
2 tablespoons all-purpose flour
1 cup 2 percent milk
1–2 teaspoons honey or sugar

GROWN-UPS
2 tablespoons chopped flat-leaf parsley or cilantro

1 green onion, minced
Salt and pepper to taste

CHILDREN
½ tablespoon butter
Salt to taste

Line a work area with wax paper or paper towels. Place a cutting board in the center of the work area. Hold the corn at a slight angle with the stalk end on the cutting board. Using a paring knife or small serrated knife, cut down from the top close to the cob, letting the kernels fall to the cutting board and surrounding work area. Set the cobs aside.

Bring 2 cups of water to a boil. *Do not add salt.* Add the corn kernels, cover, and cook over medium-high heat for 2–3 minutes, until the corn is tender. Drain the water. Scrape the cobs with a knife over the corn, letting the juice and pulp fall into the saucepan. Whisk the flour and milk together. Pour into the saucepan and stir over medium-high heat until the mixture begins to bubble and thickens. Add more milk a little at a time if the mixture becomes too thick. Stir in the honey. Transfer half to another dish.

Stir the parsley and green onions into half of the corn; season with salt and pepper. Add the butter to the remaining corn and stir until melted; season with salt, if desired.

GROWN-UPS
Calories 240; Calories from fat 30
Total fat 3.5 g; Saturated fat 1 g
Cholesterol 5 mg; Sodium 60 mg
Carbohydrate 51 g; Dietary fiber 6 g
Sugars 10 g; Protein 8 g

CHILDREN
Calories 170; Calories from fat 35
Total fat 4 g; Saturated fat 2 g
Cholesterol 10 mg; Sodium 40 mg
Carbohydrate 33 g; Dietary fiber 4 g
Sugars 7 g; Protein 5 g

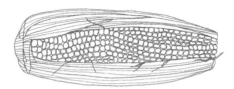

ORANGE GINGER GLAZED CARROTS
& ORANGE BUTTER GLAZED
CARROTS

Time to table: 15 minutes   Serves 2 adults and 2 children

Interesting and delicious, this versatile yet simple sauce goes well with a variety of vegetables. For the grown-ups, ginger and orange add a nice freshness to the carrots. Many children may even find this variation to their liking. This side dish goes well with Teriyaki Honey Glazed Drumsticks, Moroccan Spiced Lamb, Cajun Spiced Chicken, and Curry Baked Snapper.

1-pound package fresh baby carrots
2 tablespoons orange juice
    concentrate, thawed
1 teaspoon grated orange zest
½ teaspoon salt

GROWN-UPS
½ teaspoon grated fresh ginger

CHILDREN
½ tablespoon butter

Bring a large pot of water to a boil. Add the carrots; bring back to a boil and cook for 5–6 minutes, until tender. Drain and toss with the orange juice concentrate, orange zest, and salt. Transfer half to another dish.

Add the ginger to half of the carrots and stir to combine. Add the butter to the remaining carrots and toss until melted.

GROWN-UPS
Calories 60; Calories from fat 5
Total fat 0.5 g; Saturated fat 0 g
Cholesterol 0 mg; Sodium 330 mg
Carbohydrate 13 g; Dietary fiber 2 g
Sugars 9 g; Protein 1 g

CHILDREN
Calories 60; Calories from fat 20
Total fat 2.5 g; Saturated fat 1.5 g
Cholesterol 5 mg; Sodium 220 mg
Carbohydrate 9 g; Dietary fiber 1 g
Sugars 6 g; Protein 1 g

Orange Ginger Snap Peas: Substitute snap peas for the carrots. Cook for 1–2 minutes.

Orange Ginger Snowpeas: Substitute snowpeas for the carrots. Cook for only 45 seconds.

Orange Ginger Sweet Potatoes: Substitute mashed sweet potatoes for the carrots.

Orange Ginger Squash: Substitute mashed squash for the carrots.

THYME ROASTED CARROTS
& SIMPLY ROASTED CARROTS

Time to table: 25 minutes   Serves 2 adults and 2 or 3 children

Soft and sweet, roasted carrots are definitely worth trying. Because they are so fibrous, carrots take longer to roast than many other vegetables. Dice them very small, in about 1/2-inch-long pieces, so that they'll cook in about twenty minutes. An alternative is to use larger pieces, but increase the roasting time by 10–15 minutes. Roast the carrots in a large baking dish, keeping the pieces for the children pushed to one side. This goes well with Curried Steak With Orange Sauce, Pork Chops With Spicy Apple Chutney, and Rosemary Dijon Pork Chops.

❝I used baby carrots, which are so easy to prepare.❞

Olive oil cooking spray
1¼–1½ pounds fresh carrots,
     peeled and cut into ½-inch dice,
     about 4 cups
¼ teaspoon garlic powder
¼ teaspoon onion powder
¼ teaspoon salt

GROWN-UPS
½ teaspoon dried thyme
Freshly ground black pepper to
     taste

CHILDREN
½ tablespoon butter (optional)

Preheat oven to 450 degrees F. Coat a large baking dish with cooking spray.

Add the carrots and spray with cooking spray until lightly coated. Season the carrots with garlic powder, onion powder, and salt. Push the carrots for the children to one side of the dish. Season the remaining carrots with thyme and push to the other side of the dish. Roast for 18–20 minutes, stirring once halfway through. Season the adults' portion with pepper. Toss the children's portion with the butter, if desired, just before serving.

GROWN-UPS
Calories 70; Calories from fat 0
Total fat 0 g; Saturated fat 0 g
Cholesterol 0 mg; Sodium 55 mg
Carbohydrate 16 g; Dietary fiber 5 g
Sugars 10 g; Protein 2 g

CHILDREN
Calories 50; Calories from fat 0
Total fat 0 g; Saturated fat 0 g
Cholesterol 0 mg; Sodium 40 mg
Carbohydrate 12 g; Dietary fiber 3 g
Sugars 8 g; Protein 1 g

Thyme Roasted Sweet Potatoes: Substitute ½-inch diced sweet potatoes or yams for the carrots.

Thyme Roasted Butternut Squash: Substitute ½-inch diced squash for the carrots.

Thyme Roasted New Potatoes: Substitute ½-inch diced new potatoes for the carrots.

GARLIC MASHED POTATOES
& BUTTERY MASHED POTATOES

Time to table: 20 minutes   Serves 2 adults and 2 or 3 children

Buttery Yukon Gold potatoes are cooked in the same pot as cloves of fresh garlic. Once cooked, the garlic is removed. The potatoes for the children are mashed with butter and milk; for the grown-ups with the cooked garlic. This is great with Green Peppercorn Steak, Rosemary Dijon Pork Chops, and Lemon Rosemary Roast Chicken.

❝Most recipes for garlic mashed potatoes have you
sauté or roast the garlic as a separate step; this was
so easy. The flavor was very pronounced in the adults'
version yet subtle enough in the children's version
that they didn't complain.❞

1¼ pounds Yukon Gold potatoes,
   peeled and cut into 2-inch pieces
4 or 5 garlic cloves, peeled and tied
   in cheesecloth

GROWN-UPS
½ cup or more nonfat milk, heated
2 tablespoons chopped fresh Italian
   parsley
Salt and pepper to taste

CHILDREN
½ cup or more 2 percent milk,
   heated
½ tablespoon butter
Salt to taste

Bring 2 quarts of water to a boil. Add the potatoes and garlic. Bring
back to a boil and cook, covered, over medium-high heat until the
potatoes are tender, 6–8 minutes. Remove the garlic, drain, and separate the potatoes into adult- and children-size servings.

Remove the garlic from the cheesecloth. Mash the adult portion of
the potatoes with the garlic, adding just enough milk to reach the
desired consistency. Fold in the parsley and season with salt and pepper.

Mash the remaining potatoes and butter, adding just enough milk to
reach the desired consistency. Season with salt, if desired.

GROWN-UPS
Calories 120; Calories from fat 0
Total fat 0 g; Saturated fat 0 g
Cholesterol 0 mg; Sodium 40 mg
Carbohydrate 26 g; Dietary fiber 2 g
Sugars 5 g; Protein 5 g

CHILDREN
Calories 100; Calories from fat 25
Total fat 3 g; Saturated fat 1.5 g
Cholesterol 10 mg; Sodium 25 mg
Carbohydrate 17 g; Dietary fiber 1 g
Sugars 3 g; Protein 3 g

Pesto Mashed Potatoes: Stir in a few tablespoons of pesto sauce.

ROSEMARY ROASTED & SIMPLY
···
ROASTED NEW POTATOES
···

Time to table: 20–25 minutes   Serves 2 adults and 2 or 3 children

Silver-green, needle-leafed rosemary is perhaps one of the hardiest herbs. Rosemary springs will last for up to two weeks wrapped in plastic wrap and stored in the refrigerator. New potatoes have a crisp texture and thin skins, so peeling them is unnecessary. In this recipe, red-skinned new potatoes are roasted with highly aromatic fresh rosemary, which infuses the potatoes with undertones of lemon and pine. This dish goes well with Veal Cutlets With Fennel Mustard Sauce, Veal Scaloppini, Cajun Spiced Chicken, and Bleu Cheese Steak.

1¼ pounds new potatoes, washed and scrubbed, about 5 or 6 medium size
Olive oil cooking spray
Salt to taste

GROWN-UPS
½ tablespoon fresh rosemary, finely chopped, or 2 teaspoons dried

Freshly ground black pepper to taste

CHILDREN
½ tablespoon butter (optional)

Preheat oven to 450 degrees F. Cut the potatoes into ½-inch cubes, resulting in about 3–4 cups. Lightly coat a large baking dish with cooking spray. Add the potatoes and lightly coat with cooking spray. Season with salt.

Put the potatoes for the children to one side of the baking dish.

Sprinkle the rosemary and pepper on the potatoes for the grown-ups. Lightly stir to distribute the seasonings.

Roast for 18–20 minutes, stirring once halfway through. Arrange the potatoes for the children on their plates and place a small pat of butter on top.

GROWN-UPS
Calories 100; Calories from fat 0
Total fat 0 g; Saturated fat 0 g
Cholesterol 0 mg; Sodium 300 mg
Carbohydrate 23 g; Dietary fiber 2 g
Sugars 1 g; Protein 2 g

CHILDREN
Calories 70; Calories from fat 0
Total fat 0 g; Saturated fat 0 g
Cholesterol 0 mg; Sodium 200 mg
Carbohydrate 15 g; Dietary fiber 1 g
Sugars 1 g; Protein 1 g

Thyme Roasted New Potatoes: Substitute dried thyme for the rosemary.

LEMON MINTED PEAS
& LEMON BUTTER PEAS

Time to table: 15 minutes　　　**Serves 2 adults and 2 or 3 children**

No one will argue that fresh English peas are tender and sweet, but of all the frozen vegetables, green peas are one of the best. Considering the time saved when compared to using fresh for weeknight meals, frozen peas make a quick side dish. For the grown-ups, peas are seasoned with mint and lemon, a delightful and fresh combination. For the children, butter, mint, and lemon make a great combination. This goes well with Lemon Rosemary Roast Chicken, Baked Salmon With Pineapple Chipotle Sauce, and Orange Curry Chicken.

❝I loved being able to dress up frozen peas.❞

3–4 cups frozen peas

GROWN-UPS
*1–2 tablespoons chopped fresh
　mint
1 teaspoon grated lemon zest
1–2 tablespoons lemon juice
Salt and pepper to taste*

CHILDREN
*½ tablespoon butter
Salt to taste
1–2 tablespoons chopped fresh
　mint (optional)
½ teaspoon grated lemon zest
　(optional)*

Heat the peas according to the package directions. Drain and transfer half to another dish.

Add the mint, lemon zest, and lemon juice to half of the peas. Season with salt and pepper.

Add the butter to the other half and stir until melted. Season with salt, if desired. Fold in the mint and lemon zest, if desired.

GROWN-UPS
Calories 100; Calories from fat 0
Total fat 0 g; Saturated fat 0 g
Cholesterol 0 mg; Sodium 105 mg
Carbohydrate 19 g; Dietary fiber 7 g
Sugars 7 g; Protein 6 g

CHILDREN
Calories 80; Calories from fat 20
Total fat 2 g; Saturated fat 1 g
Cholesterol 5 mg; Sodium 70 mg
Carbohydrate 11 g; Dietary fiber 4 g
Sugars 4 g; Protein 4 g

Lemon Parsley Peas: Substitute chopped parsley for the mint.

ORANGE SESAME SNOWPEAS
& ORANGE SNOWPEAS

Time to table: 15 minutes   Serves 2 adults and 2 or 3 children

Snowpeas are entirely edible, including the pod. When cooked, the pod becomes bright green in color. The outer pod is thin and crisp while the tiny peas inside are tender and sweet. To prepare, break off the stem end and pull down the length of the pod to remove the tough string. This delicate vegetable requires very little cooking, making snowpeas particularly suitable for microwave preparation. This side dish goes well with Teriyaki Honey Glazed Drumsticks, Shanghai Chicken Kabobs, and Curry Baked Snapper.

❝We loved the orange and sesame seeds.
Wonderful combination of flavors. For vegetables,
the kids liked it.❞

1¼ pounds snowpeas, washed and trimmed

2 tablespoons orange juice concentrate, thawed

2 teaspoons grated orange zest

GROWN-UPS

1 teaspoon dark sesame oil

2 teaspoons toasted sesame seeds

Salt and pepper to taste

CHILDREN

½ tablespoon butter, cut into small pieces

Salt to taste

Toasted sesame seeds (optional)

Place the snowpeas in a microwave-safe dish with a few tablespoons of water. Cover with vented plastic wrap. Microwave at full power for 3 minutes. Alternatively, bring 2 quarts of water to a boil. Add the snowpeas and cook, uncovered, until crisp but tender, about 1 minute. Drain.

Add the orange juice concentrate and orange zest to the snowpeas, stirring to combine.

Transfer half to another dish.

To half of the snowpeas, stir in the sesame oil and sesame seeds. Season with salt and pepper.

Add the butter to the other half, and stir until melted. Season with salt, if desired, and garnish with sesame seeds.

GROWN-UPS

Calories 80; Calories from fat 35
Total fat 3.5 g; Saturated fat 0.5 g
Cholesterol 0 mg; Sodium 0 mg
Carbohydrate 9 g; Dietary fiber 2 g
Sugars 6 g; Protein 2 g

CHILDREN

Calories 60; Calories from fat 20
Total fat 2 g; Saturated fat 1 g
Cholesterol 5 mg; Sodium 0 mg
Carbohydrate 8 g; Dietary fiber 2 g
Sugars 5 g; Protein 2 g

LEMON WALNUT SNAP PEAS
& LEMONY SNAP PEAS

Time to table: 15 minutes   Serves 2 adults and 2 or 3 children

Sugar snap peas are entirely edible, including the pod. Almost the thickness of string beans, snap peas range in length from 2 to 2-1/2 inches. Sweet and crisp, snap peas are one of the most prized of all legumes. To toast the walnuts, place them in a nonstick skillet over medium-high heat, shaking frequently for 5–10 minutes; or toast in the oven for 10–15 minutes at 350 degrees F., stirring occasionally. This dish goes well with Veal Scaloppini, Chicken With Capers and Sun-Dried Tomatoes, and Steak With Madeira Mushroom Sauce.

> ❝I've never tried snap peas before. They were delicious, very sweet. I especially enjoyed the lemon and walnut flavor.❞

1¼ pounds snap peas, rinsed and
    trimmed
2 teaspoons lemon zest
2 tablespoons lemon juice

GROWN-UPS
2 tablespoons chopped toasted
    walnuts
Salt and pepper to taste

CHILDREN
½ tablespoon unsalted butter, cut
    into pieces
Salt to taste

Bring 2 quarts of water to a boil. Add the snap peas and cook until crisp tender, 2–3 minutes. Drain. Alternatively, cook in the microwave for 3–4 minutes until crisp tender. Toss with the lemon zest and lemon juice. Transfer half to another dish.

To the adults' servings, add the toasted walnuts; stir to combine. Season with salt and pepper.

To the children's servings, add the butter and stir until melted. Season with salt, if desired.

GROWN-UPS
Calories 100; Calories from fat 40
Total fat 4.5 g; Saturated fat 0 g
Cholesterol 0 mg; Sodium 10 mg
Carbohydrate 11 g; Dietary fiber 4 g
Sugars 4 g; Protein 5 g

CHILDREN
Calories 50; Calories from fat 20
Total fat 2 g; Saturated fat 1 g
Cholesterol 5 mg; Sodium 10 mg
Carbohydrate 7 g; Dietary fiber 2 g
Sugars 3 g; Protein 2 g

Lemon Walnut Green Beans: Substitute green beans for the snap peas.
Lemon Walnut English Peas: Substitute peas for the snap peas.

CARDAMOM SPICED BUTTERNUT SQUASH & CINNAMON SPICED BUTTERNUT SQUASH

Time to table: 20 minutes   **Serves 2 adults and 2 to 4 children**

In this recipe, texture plays an important role. Butternut squash is grated, then cooked in the microwave, preserving the crisp and crunchy texture. Apple and fresh lemon juice balance the flavors. For the grown-ups, the squash is seasoned with aromatic cardamom and coriander. For the children, its natural sweetness is accented with honey and cinnamon.

About cutting winter squash: The outer skin of winter squash tends to be very tough and therefore a challenge to cut open safely. Pierce the skin in several places with a knife and microwave at full power for 4–5 minutes. The skin and pulp will soften just enough to make cutting easier. Place the squash on a cutting board and pierce the center of the squash with the tip of a sturdy chef's knife, plunging it through to the other side. Applying pressure, bring the knife down from the center to one end of the squash. Repeat on the other side to cut the squash in half.

This goes well with Rosemary Dijon Pork Chops, Bayou Baked Fish, and Lemon Rosemary Roast Chicken.

"I loved the texture. Crunchy, not mushy."

½ medium-size butternut squash,
  about 2 pounds
⅓ cup apple juice
1 tablespoon fresh lemon juice

GROWN-UPS
1 teaspoon ground coriander
¹⁄₁₆ teaspoon ground cardamom or
  cloves
Salt and cayenne pepper to taste

CHILDREN
½ tablespoon honey
¼ teaspoon cinnamon or nutmeg
½ tablespoon butter (optional)
Salt to taste

Slice the squash in half lengthwise; scoop out the pulp and seeds. Peel the squash with a sturdy vegetable peeler. Cut into pieces that fit the feeding tube of your food processor. Using the largest grating disk of the processor, grate the squash. You should have about 4 cups.

Transfer the squash to a large microwave-safe dish. Pour the apple and lemon juice over the squash and toss to combine. Microwave at full power for 6 minutes, rotating the dish halfway through. Transfer half to another dish.

Stir the coriander and cardamom into half of the squash. Season with salt and cayenne pepper.

To the remaining squash, add the honey, cinnamon, and butter, if using. Stir to combine. Season with salt, if desired.

GROWN-UPS
Calories 80; Calories from fat 0
Total fat 0 g; Saturated fat 0 g
Cholesterol 0 mg; Sodium 5 mg
Carbohydrate 20 g; Dietary fiber 5 g
Sugars 6 g; Protein 2 g

CHILDREN
Calories 80; Calories from fat 20
Total fat 2 g; Saturated fat 1 g
Cholesterol 5 mg; Sodium 5 mg
Carbohydrate 16 g; Dietary fiber 3 g
Sugars 7 g; Protein 1 g

HONEY MUSTARD ACORN SQUASH
& HONEY ACORN SQUASH

Time to table: 20 minutes   Serves 2 adults and 2 or 3 children

This is a quick and simple way to prepare acorn squash. For the grown-ups, the squash is mixed with honey Dijon. Savory and sweet, the flavors are well balanced. For the children, honey and butter accentuate the natural sweetness. This is a great way to dress up frozen squash, too, and goes well with Moroccan Spiced Lamb, Green Peppercorn Steak, and Lemon Rosemary Roast Chicken.

❝*My husband and I really liked this—so simple.*❞

1 large acorn squash, about
   1¾–2 pounds

GROWN-UPS
2 tablespoons honey mustard or
   sweet hot mustard
Salt and pepper to taste

CHILDREN
1 tablespoon honey
½ tablespoon butter
Salt to taste

Cut the squash in half lengthwise and scoop out the seeds. Place cut side up in a microwave-safe dish. Cover with plastic wrap and microwave at full power for 10–12 minutes, rotating the dish halfway through. Scoop out the pulp and divide in half.

Stir the honey mustard into half of the squash. Season with salt and pepper. Stir the honey and butter into the other half of the squash. Season with salt, if desired.

GROWN-UPS
Calories 80; Calories from fat 5
Total fat 1 g; Saturated fat 0 g
Cholesterol 0 mg; Sodium 190 mg
Carbohydrate 21 g; Dietary fiber 2 g
Sugars 11 g; Protein 1 g

CHILDREN
Calories 70; Calories from fat 20
Total fat 2 g; Saturated fat 1 g
Cholesterol 5 mg; Sodium 5 mg
Carbohydrate 13 g; Dietary fiber 1 g
Sugars 7 g; Protein 1 g

Honey Mustard Sweet Potatoes: Substitute 2 or 3 cups of mashed sweet potatoes for the squash.

ITALIAN HERBED BROILED
....
TOMATOES & PARMESAN CHEESE
....
BROILED TOMATOES
....

Time to table: 10 minutes   Serves 2 adults and 2 to 4 children

Most home cooks overlook the use of tomatoes as a vegetable side dish. This simple and elegant-looking dish takes just minutes to prepare. Fresh tomatoes are lightly seasoned with Parmesan cheese and herbs, then broiled. Because tomatoes are so fragile, just a few short minutes is all that is required. This goes well with Lemon Thyme Pacific Cod, Bleu Cheese Steak, and Grilled Greek Chicken With Feta Sauce.

> ❝ *I've never tried tomatoes as a side dish.*
> *This is good.* ❞

4 small to medium-size ripe
    tomatoes
¼ cup grated Parmesan cheese
¼ teaspoon salt
¼ teaspoon garlic powder
¼ teaspoon onion powder

GROWN-UPS
Freshly ground black pepper to
    taste
½ *teaspoon Italian seasoning*

Set oven to broil.

Slice tomatoes in half crosswise. With your fingers, scoop out the seeds, leaving the chambers intact. Sprinkle the Parmesan cheese evenly over the tomatoes, gently pushing it inside the cavities. Season with salt, garlic powder, and onion powder, omitting any that the children find objectionable. Place the tomatoes for the children on a broiler pan, cut side up. Season the tomatoes for the grown-ups with pepper and Italian seasoning. Transfer to the broiler pan.

Broil the tomatoes for 3–5 minutes, until well heated and the cheese is light brown.

GROWN-UPS
Calories 60; Calories from fat 20
Total fat 2.5 g; Saturated fat 1.5 g
Cholesterol 5 mg; Sodium 130 mg
Carbohydrate 8 g; Dietary fiber 2 g
Sugars 5 g; Protein 4 g

CHILDREN
Calories 30; Calories from fat 10
Total fat 1 g; Saturated fat 0.5 g
Cholesterol 0 mg; Sodium 65 mg
Carbohydrate 4 g; Dietary fiber 1 g
Sugars 2 g; Protein 2 g

Note about storing tomatoes: Always store fresh tomatoes at room temperature (above 55 degrees F.). Never refrigerate them; cool temperatures destroy the flavor and texture. To hasten the ripening of underripe tomatoes, place them in a paper bag along with an apple or banana. The ethylene gas produced by the fruit will speed the ripening process.

Feta and Oregano Broiled Tomatoes: Substitute feta cheese for the Parmesan and dried oregano for the Italian seasoning.

CAJUN FRIED ZUCCHINI
& CRISP FRIED ZUCCHINI

Time to table: 30 minutes   **Serves 2 adults and 2 to 4 children**

Zucchini is cut into sticks and coated with a crunchy crust, then oven-"fried" until crisp on the outside and soft on the inside. For the grown-ups, a spicy mixture of tomato ketchup and hot Chinese mustard is used as the base to which the coating adheres. For the children, sweet tomato ketchup makes the coating stick. This recipe goes well with Chicken in Chipotle Chile Barbecue Sauce, Chicken Puttanesca, and Grilled Greek Chicken With Feta Sauce.

> *Zucchini has never been a family favorite. I was reluctant to test the recipe. The results really surprised us all. I loved it and couldn't stop eating it. The kids really liked it, too.*

3–4 small zucchini
3 cups cornflakes
Olive oil cooking spray
Ketchup and Chinese-style
  mustard for dipping (optional)

GROWN-UPS
2 teaspoons Cajun-style seasoning

1–2 tablespoons ketchup
1½ teaspoons Chinese-style
  mustard, extra hot

CHILDREN
1–2 tablespoons ketchup

Preheat oven to 450 degrees F. Coat a large baking sheet with cooking spray and set aside.

Rinse the zucchini under cold water, dry, and trim both ends. Cut the zucchini in half lengthwise and then into quarters. Place the cornflakes in a heavy-duty plastic bag. Squeeze out the excess air and seal. Crush the cornflakes with a rolling pin. Pour the crushed flakes into a pie pan.

Spread a thin layer of ketchup on the cut sides of the zucchini for the children. Place the zucchini into the cornflake crumbs and press the coating until it adheres. Place the zucchini, crumb side up, on the baking sheet.

Add the Cajun seasoning to the cornflakes. Mix the ketchup and mustard together in a small bowl. Spread a thin layer of the mixture on the cut sides of the zucchini for the grown-ups. Place the zucchini into the crumb mixture and press the coating until it adheres. Place the zucchini, crumb side up, on the prepared baking sheet.

When all the zucchini pieces have been coated with cornflakes, lightly spray with cooking spray. Place the baking sheet in the oven and bake until crisp on the outside and soft on the inside, 15–20 minutes. Serve immediately with more ketchup or Chinese mustard for dipping.

Note: Commercial Cajun spice mixes can be found in the spice section at the supermarket. To make your own, combine 3 tablespoons sweet paprika, 2 teaspoons onion powder, 2 teaspoons garlic powder, 2 teaspoons ground black pepper, 2 teaspoons ground white pepper, 2 teaspoons cayenne, 1 teaspoon celery salt, 1 teaspoon ground oregano, and 1 teaspoon ground thyme. This makes about ⅓ cup. Store in a tightly covered container.

GROWN-UPS
Calories 70; Calories from fat 0
Total fat 0 g; Saturated fat 0 g
Cholesterol 0 mg; Sodium 320 mg
Carbohydrate 17 g; Dietary fiber 0 g
Sugars 3 g; Protein 2 g

CHILDREN
Calories 45; Calories from fat 0
Total fat 0 g; Saturated fat 0 g
Cholesterol 0 mg; Sodium 210 mg
Carbohydrate 10 g; Dietary fiber 0 g
Sugars 2 g; Protein 1 g

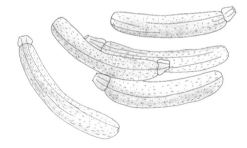

THE MAIN EVENT

Main Course Salads and
Meat, Poultry, Seafood, and
Vegetable Main Dishes

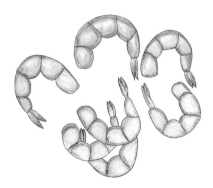

MAIN COURSE SALADS

....

WILTED SPINACH SALAD
....

& SHRIMP SALAD
....

Time to table: 25 minutes   Serves 2 adults and 2 children

This salad can be assembled in no time using prewashed packaged spinach. While I still rinse the leaves in cold water and spin dry, much of the time-consuming task of ridding fresh spinach of sandy soil is eliminated. For the grown-ups, a bed of spinach lines the plate. Fresh tomatoes, tiny shrimp, and chopped egg whites complete the presentation. The color contrast is beautiful. A warm smoky-flavored bacon dressing finishes the salad. For the children, substitute iceberg lettuce for spinach and arrange the salads with the ingredients separated, if desired.

5–6 cups spinach leaves, torn into
  bite-size pieces
4 hardboiled eggs
4 ripe tomatoes, cut into wedges
¾ pound cooked tiny shrimp

GROWN-UPS
Warm Bacon Dressing
  (recipe follows)

CHILDREN
4 cups iceberg lettuce, torn into
  pieces
¼ cup ranch dressing or other
  favorite, low-fat or regular

Peel the hardboiled eggs. Slice 2 of the eggs in half and discard the yolk. Chop the egg white and set aside. Slice the remaining eggs.

Arrange the salads for the grown-ups using the spinach, tomatoes, chopped egg whites, and shrimp. Serve with Warm Bacon Dressing.

Arrange the salad for the children using the lettuce, tomatoes, sliced eggs, and shrimp, omitting any that they might dislike. Serve with ranch dressing.

❝I assembled the children's salads on a large dinner plate. In the center, I placed two egg slices for eyes. The nose was made out of shrimp in a triangular design and tomato wedges for the mouth. I chopped spinach and used it for hair around the edge of the plate. The kids were delighted and even ate some of the spinach.❞

WARM BACON DRESSING

½ tablespoon extra-virgin olive oil
¼ cup finely chopped Canadian
  bacon, about 3 slices
¼ cup finely chopped shallots

¼ cup rice vinegar
Freshly ground black pepper
  to taste

Heat the oil in a nonstick skillet over medium-high heat for 2 minutes. Add the Canadian bacon and shallots. Stir for several minutes until the shallots begin to brown. Reduce heat to low and cook for 5 minutes. Add the vinegar to the pan, scraping the bottom with a spatula to loosen any browned bits. Season to taste with pepper. Serve immediately.

GROWN-UPS
Calories 200; Calories from fat 50
Total fat 5 g; Saturated fat 0.5 g
Cholesterol 185 mg; Sodium 490 mg
Carbohydrate 11 g; Dietary fiber 3 g
Sugars 5 g; Protein 33 g

CHILDREN
Calories 190; Calories from fat 60
Total fat 7 g; Saturated fat 0 g
Cholesterol 165 mg; Sodium 510 mg
Carbohydrate 9 g; Dietary fiber 3 g
Sugars 4 g; Protein 25 g

ITALIAN ANTIPASTO SALAD

& ITALIAN VEGETABLE SALAD

Time to table: 20 minutes   Serves 2 adults and 2 or 3 children

This is a hearty dinner salad with endless variations. Use any combination of vegetables that the children like. Zucchini, yellow squash, blanched asparagus, broccoli, marinated artichoke hearts, or mushrooms would also make great additions to this salad. For a gourmet touch, use fresh mozzarella cheese and prosciutto instead of ham. For the children, you may want to arrange the salad ingredients separately on the plate. Substitute iceberg lettuce if they prefer it, and let them use their favorite salad dressing.

This salad is easy to do and easily adaptable; I can just include the vegetables that my kids like.

5–6 cups mixed salad greens
2 large ripe tomatoes, cut into wedges
1 medium cucumber, peeled and diced
1 red bell pepper, cored and sliced
1 15½-ounce can garbanzo beans, rinsed and drained
2 ounces diced mozzarella cheese
4 ounces lean ham or Canadian bacon, diced

8–10 pitted Greek olives

GROWN-UPS
2 or 3 pickled pepperoncini peppers, quartered
2 or 3 thin slices of red onion
Italian Vinaigrette (recipe follows)

CHILDREN
¼ cup creamy Italian dressing or other favorite, low-fat or regular

Arrange the salad greens on four dinner plates. Arrange the tomatoes, cucumbers, bell peppers, garbanzo beans, mozzarella, ham, and olives attractively on the plates, omitting any that the children might dislike.

Arrange the pepperoncini peppers and red onions on the salads for the grown-ups and serve with Italian Vinaigrette.

Serve the salads for the children with creamy Italian dressing.

ITALIAN VINAIGRETTE

½ teaspoon Dijon mustard
½ tablespoon extra-virgin olive oil
½ tablespoon red wine vinegar
2 teaspoons minced shallots
1 garlic clove, minced

2 tablespoons strained applesauce
 (baby food)
½ teaspoon crumbled oregano
Salt and freshly ground black
 pepper to taste

Spoon the mustard into the bottom of a small bowl. Whisk the olive oil into the mustard with a small wire whisk until fully blended. Whisk in the red wine vinegar, shallots, garlic, applesauce, and oregano. Season with salt and freshly ground black pepper.

GROWN-UPS
Calories 330; Calories from fat 110
Total fat 12 g; Saturated fat 3 g
Cholesterol 35 mg; Sodium 420 mg
Carbohydrate 34 g; Dietary fiber 9 g
Sugars 7 g; Protein 23 g

CHILDREN
Calories 210; Calories from fat 70
Total fat 8 g; Saturated fat 2 g
Cholesterol 25 mg; Sodium 320 mg
Carbohydrate 22 g; Dietary fiber 6 g
Sugars 4 g; Protein 15 g

WARM CHICKEN TERIYAKI SALAD
& WARM PINEAPPLE CHICKEN SALAD

Time to table: 30 minutes   Serves 2 adults and 2 children

Warm main course salads can be served any time of the year. Here chicken, pineapple, peppers, and onions are glazed with teriyaki sauce and grilled or broiled. For the grown-ups, a pineapple teriyaki dressing is made to accentuate the pineapple flavor. For the children, use dark meat if they have a preference and omit the teriyaki sauce from their portions if not to their liking. Since many children prefer that their food "not touch," arrange the salad ingredients on the plate separately with the dressing on the side.

❝Terrific warm or cold. Tasty, colorful, and low in fat.❞

½ cup or more thick teriyaki sauce
1 pound boneless and skinless
  chicken (breast meat or thighs)
4 slices fresh pineapple
1 medium red or green pepper,
  seeded, cored, and cut into strips
1 medium yellow onion, cut into
  slices and secured with
  toothpicks (see note)

6 cups mixed salad greens
Pineapple Teriyaki Dressing
  (recipe follows)

GROWN-UPS
2 green onions, sliced, for garnish

Set oven to broil or start the coals of an outdoor barbecue.

If using chicken breasts, remove the tenderloin, the small strip of meat on the rib side of the breast, and cook separately. If the chicken breasts are very thick, pound the thickest part between sheets of plastic wrap with the flat side of a meat tenderizer. (This will ensure that the chicken cooks quickly; if time is not important, you can skip these steps.) Brush the chicken, pineapple slices, red pepper, and onions with teriyaki sauce. Broil or grill the chicken until no longer pink in the center, 5–6 minutes per side, and until the pineapple, peppers, and onions are tender. Transfer to a cutting board and cut the chicken into thin slices. Cut the pineapple slices into wedges, the peppers into 2-inch pieces, and separate the onion slices into rings.

Arrange the salad greens on four dinner plates. Arrange the chicken, pineapple, red peppers, and onions on the plates, omitting any that the children might dislike. Garnish the salads for the grown-ups with green onions. Serve with Pineapple Teriyaki Dressing.

Note: After slicing the onions, put a toothpick into each slice to keep the onion from falling apart while cooking. Remove the toothpick before serving.

PINEAPPLE TERIYAKI DRESSING

½ cup pineapple juice
½ tablespoon light soy sauce
2 garlic cloves, minced
1–2 green onions, minced

½ tablespoon dark sesame oil
2 tablespoons strained applesauce
   (baby food)
1 teaspoon honey

Combine the pineapple juice, soy sauce, garlic, onions, sesame oil, applesauce, and honey.

GROWN-UPS
Calories 320; Calories from fat 50
Total fat 6 g; Saturated fat 1 g
Cholesterol 65 mg; Sodium 510 mg
Carbohydrate 38 g; Dietary fiber 5 g
Sugars 29 g; Protein 30 g

CHILDREN
Calories 320; Calories from fat 50
Total fat 6 g; Saturated fat 1 g
Cholesterol 65 mg; Sodium 510 mg
Carbohydrate 38 g; Dietary fiber 5 g
Sugars 29 g; Protein 30 g

CHINESE CHICKEN SALAD &
CHICKEN AND ORANGE SALAD

Time to table: 20 minutes   **Serves 2 adults and 2 children**

For this salad, use a lettuce that has some crunch to it. Iceberg or romaine are good choices. The salad dressing is a sweet-tart mixture of orange juice and rice vinegar seasoned with ginger. For the children, arrange everything on the dinner plate separately with the dressing in a small bowl. Sometimes after tasting the ingredients, the children might decide to mix them all together themselves.

❝I used deli roasted chicken—very easy, good, and healthy tasting. We all loved the Orange Sesame Dressing.❞

1 pound boneless and skinless
   chicken breast or thighs,
   or substitute 1½ cups cooked
   diced chicken
¼ teaspoon of each: salt, garlic
   powder, and onion powder
5–6 cups shredded lettuce
1 3-ounce can chow mein noodles

GROWN-UPS
2–3 green onions, sliced on the

diagonal
15 sprigs cilantro, stems removed
Orange Sesame Dressing
   (recipe follows)

CHILDREN
1 10½-ounce can mandarin
   oranges, drained
Orange Ginger Dressing
   (recipe follows)

Season the chicken with salt, garlic powder, and onion powder, omitting any that the children dislike. If using chicken breasts, remove the tenderloin, the small strip of meat on the rib side of the breast, and cook separately. If the breasts are thick, pound the thickest part between sheets of plastic wrap with the flat side of a meat tenderizer. (This ensures that the chicken cooks quickly; if time is not important, you can skip these steps.) Heat a nonstick skillet for 2 minutes over medium-high heat. Pan-fry the chicken for 5–6 minutes on each side or until cooked through. Remove from the pan and cut into thin slices.

While the chicken is cooking, arrange the lettuce on four dinner plates. To assemble the salads for the grown-ups, sprinkle ½ cup of chow mein noodles, the green onions, and cilantro on each of the salads. Place the chicken on top and serve with Orange Sesame Dressing.

To assemble the salads for the children, sprinkle the remaining chow mein noodles and the mandarin oranges over the salads. Place the chicken on top and serve with Orange Ginger Dressing.

ORANGE SESAME DRESSING

¼ cup orange juice concentrate,
   thawed
2 tablespoons rice vinegar
2 teaspoons light soy sauce
½ tablespoon dark sesame oil

1 garlic clove, minced
½–1 teaspoon grated fresh ginger
   or ½ teaspoon dried
2 teaspoons toasted sesame seeds

Combine all the ingredients in a small bowl.

ORANGE GINGER DRESSING

¼ cup orange juice concentrate
1 tablespoon rice vinegar
½ teaspoon grated fresh ginger
   or ¼ teaspoon dried

½ tablespoon light soy sauce
   (optional)

Combine all the ingredients in a small bowl.

GROWN-UPS
Calories 310; Calories from fat 90
Total fat 10 g; Saturated fat 2 g
Cholesterol 65 mg; Sodium 410 mg
Carbohydrate 25 g; Dietary fiber 2 g
Sugars 14 g; Protein 29 g

CHILDREN
Calories 330; Calories from fat 80
Total fat 9 g; Saturated fat 1.5 g
Cholesterol 65 mg; Sodium 210 mg
Carbohydrate 34 g; Dietary fiber 2 g
Sugars 24 g; Protein 29 g

CHICKEN CAESAR SALAD
& CHICKEN SALAD

Time to table: 20–25 minutes   **Serves 2 adults and 2 or 3 children**

As far as I'm concerned, the best part of a Caesar salad is the dressing, classically a savory blend of garlic, anchovies, Parmesan cheese, lemon juice, and raw egg. Food safety experts warn against the use of raw eggs because of the potential for causing illness. My variation is safe to eat and delicious, too. The basic process involves cooking the eggs in the top of a double boiler for 3 minutes. The trick is to keep the eggs moving swiftly so that they never get a chance to set. The eggs become thick and creamy, giving the dressing good body without the need for a lot of oil. For those of you who don't want to be bothered, I've also included another dressing that's quick and easy. Use anchovy fillets instead of anchovy paste for best results. Make the salad dressing first so that the flavors have time to blend.

1 pound boneless and skinless
  chicken, breast meat or thighs,
  or 1½ cups shredded cooked
  chicken
¼ teaspoon of each: salt, garlic
  powder, and onion powder
6 cups romaine lettuce, rinsed and
  torn into bite-size pieces
½ cup freshly shredded Parmesan
  cheese
Garlic croutons (see note)

GROWN-UPS
Classic Caesar Salad Dressing
  (recipe follows) or Quick
  Caesar Salad Dressing
  (recipe follows)
Chopped anchovy fillets for garnish

CHILDREN
¼ cup creamy Italian dressing or
  other favorite, low-fat or regular

"Loved the salad. Tried both dressings—both were good. Nice way to use deli chicken or leftovers."

Season the chicken with salt, garlic powder, and onion powder, omitting any that the children dislike. If using chicken breasts, remove the tenderloin, the small strip of meat on the rib side of the breast, and cook separately. If the breasts are thick, pound the chicken between sheets of plastic wrap with the flat side of a meat tenderizer. (This ensures that the chicken cooks quickly; if time is not important, you can skip these steps.) Heat a nonstick skillet for 2 minutes over medium-high heat. Pan-fry the chicken for 5–6 minutes on each side or until cooked through. Remove from the pan and cut into slices.

Toss the lettuce for the grown-ups with either of the dressings and half of the Parmesan cheese. Arrange the lettuce on two dinner plates. Top with the chicken. Garnish with garlic croutons and chopped anchovies, if desired.

Arrange the lettuce and chicken on the plates for the children. Scatter the remaining Parmesan on top. Serve with creamy Italian dressing and garlic croutons.

QUICK CAESAR SALAD DRESSING

6 small anchovy fillets, about half
   of a 2-ounce tin
1 garlic clove, minced
½ teaspoon sugar
¼ teaspoon black pepper

¼ teaspoon Worcestershire sauce
2 tablespoons fresh lemon juice
¼ cup mayonnaise, low-fat or
   reduced-fat

Drain and rinse the anchovies. Pat dry on paper towels and mash with a fork to make a paste. Combine the paste with the garlic, sugar, black pepper, Worcestershire sauce, lemon juice, and mayonnaise.

CLASSIC CAESAR SALAD DRESSING

6 small anchovy fillets, about half
   of a 2-ounce tin
1 garlic clove, minced
1 teaspoon sugar
½ teaspoon freshly ground black
   pepper
½ teaspoon Worcestershire sauce

1–2 teaspoons extra-virgin olive oil
3 tablespoons fresh lemon juice
1 egg
3 egg whites
Freshly ground black pepper
   to taste

Drain and rinse the anchovies. Pat dry on paper towels. Mash the anchovies with a fork in the bottom of a salad bowl. Add the garlic, sugar, pepper, Worcestershire sauce, olive oil, and lemon juice, and stir to combine.

Prepare an ice water bath using a large mixing bowl or the kitchen sink. Fill a saucepan with water and bring to a boil. Add the egg and egg whites to a glass bowl that fits on top of the saucepan. Scramble the eggs with a wire whisk. Place the bowl over the boiling water. Reduce heat to medium. Stir the eggs constantly for 3 minutes or until the temperature reaches 145 degrees F. on an instant-read thermometer. Do not allow the eggs to set. Transfer the bowl to the ice water bath. Continue to stir for few minutes and until the the bowl and contents have cooled.

Transfer the eggs to the anchovy mixture and stir together. Season to taste with freshly ground black pepper. Add the lettuce and Parmesan cheese, tossing to combine.

Note: Salad croutons can be purchased ready made. To make your own, cut French bread into small cubes. Coat with olive oil cooking spray. Toss with minced garlic and salt. Place on a baking sheet and bake at 350 degrees F. for 10 minutes or more, until crisp.

GROWN-UPS
Calories 350; Calories from fat 80
Total fat 9 g; Saturated fat 4.5 g
Cholesterol 95 mg; Sodium 990 mg
Carbohydrate 21 g; Dietary fiber 2 g
Sugars 3 g; Protein 40 g

CHILDREN
Calories 210; Calories from fat 60
Total fat 7 g; Saturated fat 2.5 g
Cholesterol 50 mg; Sodium 510 mg
Carbohydrate 13 g; Dietary fiber 1 g
Sugars 1 g; Protein 23 g

WARM ITALIAN SHRIMP SALAD
& WARM PARMESAN SHRIMP SALAD

Time to table: 20 minutes   **Serves 2 adults and 2 or 3 children**

Fresh shrimp are tossed with a zesty seasoning mix, then quickly sautéed and placed on a bed of greens. Buy the shrimp already peeled and deveined to make this quick and easy main course salad. Serve with garlic bread (see note) for a light supper.

6 cups spring mix or red leaf
   lettuce
4 large ripe tomatoes, chopped
1 14-ounce can artichoke hearts,
   rinsed and drained
Thin slices of red onion (optional)
1½ pounds shrimp, peeled and
   deveined

GROWN-UPS
2 teaspoons Italian seasoning
   (see note)
2 teaspoons sweet paprika
¼ teaspoon garlic powder

¼ teaspoon onion powder
Dash of cayenne pepper
¼ teaspoon salt
1 teaspoon grated lemon zest
Italian Vinaigrette (page 88)

CHILDREN
⅛ teaspoon salt
¼ teaspoon garlic powder
2 tablespoons grated Parmesan
   cheese
¼ cup creamy Italian dressing or
   other favorite, low-fat or regular

Arrange the spring mix, tomatoes, and artichoke hearts attractively on four dinner plates, omitting any ingredients that the children dislike. Arrange the sliced onions on the plates for the grown-ups.

Divide the shrimp in half. Season the shrimp for the children with salt and garlic powder, if desired. Heat a nonstick skillet for 2 minutes. Add the shrimp and cook for 2–3 minutes, until no longer translucent in the center. Arrange on the salads for the children. Sprinkle with Parmesan cheese and serve with creamy Italian dressing.

Mix the Italian seasoning, paprika, garlic powder, onion powder, cayenne pepper, salt, and lemon zest together in a medium-size bowl. Add the remaining shrimp and toss until the seasonings are evenly distributed.

Heat the skillet for 2 minutes and cook the shrimp over medium-high heat for 2–3 minutes, until no longer translucent in the center.

Arrange on the salads for the grown-ups and serve with Italian Vinaigrette.

Note: To make a simple garlic bread, slice French bread in half. Broil until browned. Rub peeled garlic over the bread. The toasted surface acts like sandpaper, leaving behind finely grated garlic. Brush with a little melted butter, if desired.

Italian seasoning is a blend of oregano, sage, rosemary, savory, thyme, and basil available already mixed in the spice section of most supermarkets.

GROWN-UPS
Calories 260; Calories from fat 60
Total fat 6 g; Saturated fat 1 g
Cholesterol 240 mg; Sodium 990 mg
Carbohydrate 23 g; Dietary fiber 9 g
Sugars 6 g; Protein 31 g

CHILDREN
Calories 190; Calories from fat 50
Total fat 5 g; Saturated fat 1.5 g
Cholesterol 165 mg; Sodium 720 mg
Carbohydrate 15 g; Dietary fiber 6 g
Sugars 4 g; Protein 22 g

THAI BEEF SALAD & BEEF SALAD

. . . .

Time to table: 30 minutes   Serves 2 adults and 2 or 3 children

L ondon broil is cut into thin slices, seasoned with lime juice, and
pan-fried. Once cooked, the warm beef is arranged on a bed of
greens. The colorful contrast between the bright orange carrots and
green salad is visually appealing. For the grown-ups, a tart salad dressing is made with lime juice and fresh herbs, including mint and
cilantro, with a little red pepper thrown in for zip. For the children, the
steak, tomatoes, and cucumbers may be arranged separately on the
dinner plate. Serve with more traditional thousand island dressing or
other favorite dressing.

❝*Really great salad! The dressing was good; we*
loved the flavors of lime, cilantro, and mint together.
The kids liked the meat.❞

6 cups salad greens
2 carrots, peeled and grated, about
  ½–¾ cup
¼ cup torn mint leaves
1 pound London broil, cut into
  thin slices
2 tablespoons fresh lime juice
¼ teaspoon salt
⅛ teaspoon freshly ground black
  pepper (or more)
½ teaspoon garlic powder

GROWN-UPS
2 green onions, cut into 2-inch
  lengths and slivered
¼ cup chopped cilantro
Thai Dressing (recipe follows)

CHILDREN
5–10 cherry tomatoes
½ cucumber, peeled and diced
¼ cup thousand island dressing or
  other favorite, low-fat or regular

Arrange the salad greens, grated carrots, and mint on four dinner
plates, omitting any ingredients that the children dislike. Season the
steak with the lime juice, salt, pepper, and garlic powder. Heat a nonstick skillet over high heat for 2 minutes. Add the steak and stir-fry for
3–4 minutes, until cooked through.

For the grown-ups, add the green onions and cilantro to the salads.
Top with warm steak and serve with Thai Dressing.

For the children, place the steak on the plates. Arrange the tomatoes and cucumbers. Serve with favored dressing.

THAI DRESSING

½ teaspoon grated lime zest
3 tablespoons fresh lime juice
2 tablespoons rice vinegar
1 tablespoon chopped fresh mint
1 tablespoon chopped fresh cilantro

1 green onion, minced
2 garlic cloves, minced
¼ teaspoon red pepper flakes
Salt to taste

In a small bowl, combine the lime zest, lime juice, rice vinegar, mint, cilantro, onions, garlic, and red pepper flakes. Season with salt.

GROWN-UPS
Calories 280; Calories from fat 110
Total fat 12 g; Saturated fat 5 g
Cholesterol 75 mg; Sodium 130 mg
Carbohydrate 11 g; Dietary fiber 3 g
Sugars 5 g; Protein 33 g

CHILDREN
Calories 220; Calories from fat 90
Total fat 9 g; Saturated fat 4 g
Cholesterol 55 mg; Sodium 170 mg
Carbohydrate 11 g; Dietary fiber 3 g
Sugars 7 g; Protein 22 g

WARM TACO SALAD WITH MEXICAN
SOUR CREAM DRESSING & WARM
TACO SALAD WITH RANCH DRESSING

Time to table: 25 minutes   Serves 2 adults and 2 or 3 children

Ground turkey breast replaces traditional ground beef in this taco salad, cutting the calories from fat considerably. The turkey is browned with taco seasoning for flavor—though chili powder, garlic powder, and onion powder with a touch of oregano could be used if you are trying to limit salt. Fresh tomatoes, cucumbers, green onions, and black beans along with a little grated Cheddar cheese complete the salad. As a garnish, crumbled tortilla chips add crunch and texture. Serve with warm flour tortillas to complete the meal.

1 pound lean ground turkey
    breast
2 tablespoons taco seasoning
5–6 cups mixed salad greens
2–3 tomatoes, chopped
1 medium cucumber, diced
3–4 green onions, sliced
1 cup grated reduced-fat or regular
    cheese, Cheddar or Monterey
    Jack

1 15-ounce can black beans,
    rinsed and drained
10–12 corn chips, crumbled

GROWN-UPS
Mexican Sour Cream Dressing
    (recipe follows)

CHILDREN
¼ cup ranch dressing or other
    favorite, low-fat or regular

Heat a nonstick skillet over medium-high heat for 2 minutes. Season the turkey with taco seasoning and brown, breaking into small pieces. (If the children dislike taco seasoning, brown half of the turkey without it; then season the rest with 1 tablespoon of the taco seasoning and brown.)

Arrange the salad greens, tomatoes, cucumber, green onions, cheese, beans, and corn chips on four dinner plates, omitting any ingredients that the children dislike.

Divide the turkey mixture among the four plates. Top the salads for grown-ups with Mexican Dressing. Top the salads for children with ranch dressing.

MEXICAN SOUR CREAM DRESSING

¼ cup nonfat or reduced-fat sour
    cream
2 teaspoons taco seasoning

2 tablespoons tomato salsa
1 tablespoon rice vinegar

Mix the sour cream, taco seasoning, salsa, and vinegar together in a small bowl.

GROWN-UPS
Calories 380; Calories from fat 45
Total fat 5 g; Saturated fat 2 g
Cholesterol 80 mg; Sodium 780 mg
Carbohydrate 38 g; Dietary fiber 10 g
Sugars 10 g; Protein 46 g

CHILDREN
Calories 300; Calories from fat 80
Total fat 9 g; Saturated fat 2.5 g
Cholesterol 55 mg; Sodium 440 mg
Carbohydrate 24 g; Dietary fiber 7 g
Sugars 6 g; Protein 29 g

GREEK SALAD & COBB SALAD

Time to table: 20 minutes   **Serves 2 adults and 2 or 3 children**

Use crisp romaine lettuce, cherry tomatoes, sun-dried tomatoes, cucumbers, and roasted red peppers in this Greek salad. A little feta cheese adds a delightful flavor, and Greek or Calamata olives are preferable to the canned variety. For the children, sliced American cheese and turkey cut into strips is altogether different from the adult version but more in line with their taste.

6 cups romaine lettuce torn into
  bite-size pieces
1 basket cherry tomatoes
¼ cup oil-packed sun-dried
  tomatoes, rinsed and chopped
1 cucumber, peeled and diced

GROWN-UPS
¼ cup chopped red onions
6–8 pitted Greek olives, halved
1 7¼-ounce jar roasted red
  peppers, rinsed, drained, and
  coarsely chopped

¼ cup crumbled feta cheese
Lemon Oregano Vinaigrette
  (recipe follows)

CHILDREN
2 slices American cheese, cut into
  ¼-inch strips
3–4 ounces turkey or ham, cut
  into ¼-inch strips
¼ cup ranch or thousand island
  dressing, low-fat or regular

Arrange the lettuce, tomatoes, and cucumber on four dinner plates, omitting any ingredients that the children dislike.

For the grown-ups, arrange the onions, olives, roasted red peppers, and feta cheese on the salads. Serve with Lemon Oregano Vinaigrette.

For the children, arrange the American cheese and turkey on the salads. Serve with ranch dressing or thousand island dressing.

LEMON OREGANO VINAIGRETTE

½ teaspoon honey Dijon mustard
½ tablespoon extra-virgin olive oil
½ teaspoon grated lemon zest
2 tablespoons fresh lemon juice
1 garlic clove, minced
2 tablespoons strained applesauce
    (baby food)

½ teaspoon crumbled oregano
⅛ teaspoon salt
½ teaspoon sugar
Freshly ground black pepper
    to taste

Whisk together the mustard and olive oil with a small wire whisk. Stir in the lemon zest, lemon juice, garlic, applesauce, oregano, salt, sugar, and black pepper.

GROWN-UPS
Calories 200; Calories from fat 90
Total fat 10 g; Saturated fat 3.5 g
Cholesterol 15 mg; Sodium 810 mg
Carbohydrate 24 g; Dietary fiber 5 g
Sugars 13 g; Protein 8 g

CHILDREN
Calories 210; Calories from fat 100
Total fat 12 g; Saturated fat 4.5 g
Cholesterol 40 mg; Sodium 480 mg
Carbohydrate 11 g; Dietary fiber 3 g
Sugars 5 g; Protein 14 g

SEAFOOD

....

Fish has received a great deal of good press lately; that's because fish contains omega-3 fatty acids, which have been found to be beneficial to coronary health—lowering "bad" LDL cholesterol and raising "good" HDL cholesterol.

Each fish has its own unique flavor, but you are free to substitute just about any type of fish in many of the following recipes. Salmon, swordfish, halibut, cod, red snapper, orange roughy, and even tuna can be used. For some children who may have a strong aversion to fish, feel free to substitute chicken. Or if they like fish sticks, keep them on hand and just heat and serve.

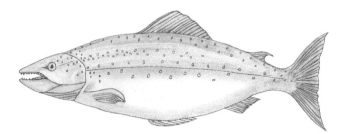

POACHED SALMON WITH DILL OR
LEMON HOLLANDAISE SAUCE

Time to table: 30 minutes   Serves 2 adults and 2 or 3 children

Salmon paired with hollandaise sauce is a classic combination. Although salmon is higher in fat than many fish, it is also a rich source of omega-3 oils, which have been found beneficial to coronary health. Poaching is a foolproof method for cooking this delicious fish. The poaching liquid can be as simple as plain water or seasoned with aromatic vegetables for more flavor. This entrée goes well with Garlic Roasted Broccoli or Asparagus, Italian Herbed Broiled Tomatoes, and Lemon Walnut Snap Peas.

❝The salmon was so good, moist and tender. I liked the hollandaise sauce.❞

FOR THE SALMON
1½ quarts water
4 lemon slices
½ cup white wine
6 peppercorns
1 teaspoon salt
1 bay leaf
2 salmon steaks, about 1½ pounds

FOR THE HOLLANDAISE
1 cup 2 percent milk
1 tablespoon cornstarch

⅛ teaspoon ground saffron
½ teaspoon salt
1 teaspoon grated lemon zest
2 tablespoons fresh lemon juice
1 tablespoon butter, cut into pieces

GROWN-UPS
2 tablespoons chopped fresh dill
Salt and pepper to taste

CHILDREN
1 tablespoon butter, cut into pieces
Salt to taste

Pour the water into a large pot. Add lemon slices, wine, pepper-corns, salt, and bay leaf. Bring to a boil and cook for 5 minutes. Add the salmon steaks, bring back to a boil, reduce heat to medium, and cook for 2 minutes. Remove from the heat, cover, and let stand for 20 minutes.

While the salmon is poaching, blend the milk, cornstarch, saffron, salt, lemon zest, and lemon juice together in a medium-size saucepan. Bring to a boil while stirring. Lower the heat to medium, and continue to cook for 1 minute. Remove from the heat. Add the butter and stir until melted. The hollandaise sauce can also be made in the microwave. Blend the milk, cornstarch, saffron, salt, lemon zest, and lemon juice together in a large-capacity microwave-safe measuring cup or glass bowl. Microwave at full power for 3–4 minutes or until the mixture reaches a boil. Whisk the sauce and microwave at full power for 1 minute longer. Whisk again, and stir in the butter until melted.

Pour half of the sauce into another dish for the children. Add the butter and stir until melted. Season with salt.

Stir the chopped dill into the remaining sauce. Season with salt and pepper.

Use a large spatula or slotted spoon to gently remove the salmon from the poaching liquid and place on individual dinner plates. Allow diners to serve themselves the hollandaise sauces.

GROWN-UPS	CHILDREN
Calories 270; Calories from fat 90	Calories 210; Calories from fat 90
Total fat 10 g; Saturated fat 3.5 g	Total fat 10 g; Saturated fat 4.5 g
Cholesterol 100 mg; Sodium 440 mg	Cholesterol 80 mg; Sodium 290 mg
Carbohydrate 6 g; Dietary fiber 0 g	Carbohydrate 4 g; Dietary fiber 0 g
Sugars 3 g; Protein 36 g	Sugars 2 g; Protein 24 g

Poached Halibut With Parsley Hollandaise Sauce: Substitute flat-leaf pars-ley for the dill and halibut for the salmon.

CHILI BAKED SALMON & BROWN

SUGAR BAKED SALMON

Time to table: 25 minutes   Serves 2 adults and 2 or 3 children

Full-flavored salmon stands up to this sweet and spicy sauce made with balsamic vinegar, brown sugar, tomato, lots of garlic, and ginger. For the grown-ups, red chili sauce turns up the heat. This entrée goes well with Lemon Minted Peas, Cilantro Quinoa Pilaf, and Lime Cilantro Pilaf.

Olive oil cooking spray
2 salmon steaks or fillets, about
   1½ pounds
⅓ cup balsamic vinegar
⅓ cup light brown sugar
¼ cup tomato paste
3 garlic cloves, minced

2 teaspoons grated fresh ginger
   or 1 teaspoon ground

GROWN-UPS
Salt and pepper to taste
1–2 teaspoons red chili sauce

CHILDREN
Salt to taste

Preheat oven to 450 degrees F. Lightly coat two small baking dishes with cooking spray. Rinse the salmon under cold water and pat dry. Season the salmon for the grown-ups with salt and pepper. Season the salmon for the children with salt, if desired.

Whisk together the balsamic vinegar, brown sugar, tomato paste, garlic, and ginger. Brush about half of the sauce over the salmon for the children and place in one of the baking dishes.

Stir in the red chili sauce to the remaining brown sugar mixture. Brush the sauce over the salmon for the grown-ups and place in the other baking dish.

Bake for 18–20 minutes or until cooked through. The salmon is done when the meat is evenly colored and flakes easily with a fork.

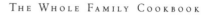

GROWN-UPS
Calories 300; Calories from fat 50
Total fat 6 g; Saturated fat 1 g
Cholesterol 90 mg; Sodium 140 mg
Carbohydrate 25 g; Dietary fiber 0 g
Sugars 21 g; Protein 35 g

CHILDREN
Calories 200; Calories from fat 35
Total fat 4 g; Saturated fat 0.5 g
Cholesterol 60 mg; Sodium 95 mg
Carbohydrate 17 g; Dietary fiber 0 g
Sugars 14 g; Protein 23 g

Chili Baked Chicken: Substitute chicken breast fillets for the salmon.

BAKED SALMON WITH PINEAPPLE CHIPOTLE SAUCE & BROWN SUGAR BAKED SALMON WITH PINEAPPLE SAUCE

Time to table: 25–30 minutes   Serves 2 adults and 2 or 3 children

The salmon is lightly seasoned with brown sugar, coriander, and paprika. Pineapple, balsamic vinegar, and orange marmalade make the base of the sweet and spicy sauce. For the grown-ups, smoky chipotle chiles are added to balance the sweetness of the sauce. If unable to find the chiles in your area, substitute ¼–½ teaspoon liquid smoke, 1–2 teaspoons chopped jarred or canned jalapeños, and 1 tablespoon of tomato paste. Side dishes to serve with this entrée include Garlic Mashed Potatoes, Saffron Garlic Orzo Risotto, and Lemon Minted Peas.

Very different from what I usually prepare. The sweet and spicy sauce was delicious.

2 salmon fillets, about 1¼ pounds

GROWN-UPS

1 teaspoon ground coriander
1 teaspoon sweet paprika

2 teaspoons brown sugar
Salt and pepper to taste

CHILDREN
2 teaspoons brown sugar

PINEAPPLE CHIPOTLE SAUCE

1 8-ounce can crushed pineapple
with juice
¼ cup balsamic vinegar
⅓ cup orange marmalade

GROWN-UPS
1–2 canned chipotle chiles,
chopped fine

Preheat oven to 450 degrees F. Lightly spray a baking dish with cooking spray. Rinse the salmon and pat dry with paper towels.

Cut the salmon for the children into strips or nuggets. Season with brown sugar and place in the baking dish.

Mix together the coriander, paprika, brown sugar, salt, and pepper in a small bowl. Rub the mixture into the salmon for the grown-ups and place in the baking dish. Bake for 20–25 minutes, until the fish flakes easily.

Combine the pineapple, vinegar, and marmalade in a small saucepan. Bring to a boil over high heat. Lower the temperature to medium and cook until the mixture has reduced by one-half, about 10 minutes.

Remove half of the pineapple sauce for the children and set aside. Stir in 1 chipotle chile to the remaining sauce. Taste for spiciness. Add the other chile, if desired, and cook for another 5 minutes.

Serve the salmon for the children with the pineapple sauce on the side. Serve the salmon for the grown-ups with the chipotle sauce brushed over the top.

Note: Salmon cooks beautifully in the microwave. Place the salmon in a microwave-safe dish and cover with plastic wrap. Microwave at full power for 5–6 minutes per pound, rotating the dish halfway through. Let stand, covered, for 3 minutes before serving.

GROWN-UPS
Calories 320; Calories from fat 60
Total fat 6 g; Saturated fat 1 g
Cholesterol 90 mg; Sodium 135 mg
Carbohydrate 31 g; Dietary fiber 0 g
Sugars 28 g; Protein 35 g

CHILDREN
Calories 210; Calories from fat 35
Total fat 4 g; Saturated fat 0.5 g
Cholesterol 60 mg; Sodium 90 mg
Carbohydrate 19 g; Dietary fiber 0 g
Sugars 19 g; Protein 23 g

Swordfish With Pineapple Chipotle Sauce: Substitute swordfish for the salmon.

SOUTHWESTERN RED SNAPPER
& RED SNAPPER WITH SALSA

Time to table: 25–30 minutes   **Serves 2 adults and 2 or 3 children**

Here, red snapper is simply seasoned and then quickly pan-fried. For the children, the snapper is topped with either salsa or Italian-style tomato sauce, whichever they prefer. For the grown-ups, the southwestern-style sauce is made with mild chiles, red bell peppers, and tomatoes. When I'm really in a hurry, I skip the homemade sauce and use stewed tomatoes with Mexican seasoning. This recipe goes well with Citrus Jicama Slaw, Mixed Citrus Salad, and Garlic Roasted Broccoli.

2 red snapper fillets, about 1¼ pounds
¼ teaspoon of each: salt, pepper, garlic powder, and onion powder

GROWN-UPS
½ teaspoon chili powder
½ teaspoon ground cumin
¼ cup chopped mild chile pepper, pasilla or Anaheim
½ cup chopped red bell pepper
½ cup chopped onion

2 garlic cloves, chopped fine
3 plum tomatoes, seeded and chopped
¼ cup white wine
2 tablespoons fresh lemon juice
Chopped cilantro for garnish

CHILDREN
½ cup mild salsa or Italian tomato sauce
Monterey Jack or Parmesan cheese for garnish

❝I used my food processor to chop the peppers, onions, and tomatoes. My prep time was just a few minutes.**❞**

Rinse the snapper and pat dry. Remove any bones from the children's portion. Season the snapper with salt, pepper, garlic powder, and onion powder, omitting any that the children dislike. Season the grown-ups' portion with chili powder and cumin. Heat a nonstick skillet for 2 minutes over medium-high heat. Pan-fry the snapper for 3–4 minutes on each side or until done. Transfer to another dish.

Add the peppers, onions, garlic, tomatoes, wine, and lemon juice to the skillet. Stir to combine. Cook until the tomatoes break down and most of the liquid evaporates, about 10 minutes. Transfer the snapper for the grown-ups back to the skillet. Spoon the sauce over the fish and heat through, 2–3 minutes. Garnish with lots of cilantro.

Place the salsa or tomato sauce in a microwave-safe dish. Microwave at full power for 1 minute. Pour over the red snapper for the children. Top with Monterey Jack or Parmesan cheese.

GROWN-UPS
Calories 270; Calories from fat 30
Total fat 3 g; Saturated fat 0.5 g
Cholesterol 65 mg; Sodium 135 mg
Carbohydrate 18 g; Dietary fiber 4 g
Sugars 10 g; Protein 38 g

CHILDREN
Calories 160; Calories from fat 40
Total fat 4.5 g; Saturated fat 2 g
Cholesterol 50 mg; Sodium 400 mg
Carbohydrate 3 g; Dietary fiber 0 g
Sugars 2 g; Protein 26 g

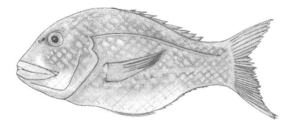

CURRY BAKED SNAPPER & ORANGE
···
BAKED SNAPPER
··

Time to table: 25 minutes   **Serves 2 adults and 2 or 3 children**

Red snapper fillets are coated with a crunchy crust then oven-baked. For the children, a hint of orange seasons the fish. For the grown-ups, a blend of curry and orange delivers a delightfully sweet and pungent flavor. A tart and savory sauce made from mango chutney, orange marmalade, and curry provides a starburst of flavor. This entrée goes well with Lime Cilantro Pilaf, Orange Ginger Glazed Carrots, and Thyme Roasted New Potatoes.

The chutney sauce was terrific.

Olive oil cooking spray
4 cup cornflakes
1 teaspoon dried orange peel
2 red snapper fillets, about 1½
   pounds

GROWN-UPS
1 teaspoon curry powder

Salt and pepper to taste
Orange Curry Chutney Sauce
   (recipe follows)

CHILDREN
Salt to taste
Mango chutney (optional)

Preheat oven to 450 degrees F. Lightly coat a baking dish with cooking spray. Place the cornflakes in a heavy-duty plastic bag. Squeeze out the excess air and seal. Finely crush the cornflakes with a rolling pin. Pour the crumbs and dried orange peel into a pie pan, stirring to combine.

Rinse the fish under cold water and pat dry. Cut the children's portions into strips and remove any bones with tweezers. Season with salt, if desired. Lightly coat the fish with cooking spray and roll in the crumb mixture until well coated. Place the fish in the baking dish and lightly spray with cooking spray.

Add the curry to the crumb mixture, stirring to combine. Season the fish for the grown-ups with salt and pepper. Lightly coat with cooking spray. Roll in the crumb mixture until well coated. Place the fish in the baking dish and lightly spray with cooking spray.

Bake the fish strips for 10–15 minutes and the fillets for 15–20 minutes or until done. Serve the strips with chutney, if acceptable, and fillets with Orange Curry Chutney Sauce.

ORANGE CURRY CHUTNEY SAUCE

½ tablespoon butter   1 tablespoon mango chutney
½ teaspoon curry powder   ½ tablespoon orange marmalade

Place the butter and curry powder in a small microwave-safe bowl. Microwave at full power until the butter is melted and bubbly, about 45–60 seconds. Stir in the chutney and marmalade. You can also melt the butter in a small saucepan; add the curry powder and cook for about 1 minute. Stir in the chutney and marmalade.

GROWN-UPS
Calories 250; Calories from fat 50
Total fat 5 g; Saturated fat 2.5 g
Cholesterol 70 mg; Sodium 190 mg
Carbohydrate 13 g; Dietary fiber 0 g
Sugars 7 g; Protein 36 g

CHILDREN
Calories 130; Calories from fat 15
Total fat 1.5 g; Saturated fat 0 g
Cholesterol 40 mg; Sodium 110 mg
Carbohydrate 4 g; Dietary fiber 0 g
Sugars 0 g; Protein 24 g

Curry Baked Chicken: Substitute boneless and skinless chicken for the red snapper.

MEDITERRANEAN GRILLED HALIBUT
& SIMPLY GRILLED HALIBUT WITH
RELISH TARTAR SAUCE

Time to table: 20–25 minutes   Serves 2 adults and 2 or 3 children

Halibut, naturally low in fat, is seasoned very simply for the children. For the grown-ups a flavorful blend of mustard seeds, fennel seeds, orange zest, and red pepper flakes is rubbed into the fish before grilling. This dish goes well with Dilly Green Beans, Italian Herbed Broiled Tomatoes, and Lemon-Herb Orzo with Feta Cheese.

*❝Nice flavor from the combination of spices,
and easy to make. I used store-bought tartar sauce
for the kids, which they like.❞*

2 halibut fillets or steaks, about 1½
   pounds
¼ teaspoon of each: salt, pepper,
   garlic powder, and onion powder
Chopped flat-leaf parsley and
   lemon wedges for garnish

GROWN-UPS
1 teaspoon mustard seeds
2 teaspoons fennel seeds

½ teaspoon dried orange peel
¼ teaspoon red pepper flakes

CHILDREN
¼ cup mayonnaise, low-fat or
   regular
2 tablespoons sweet pickle relish
½ teaspoon celery salt

Rinse the fish and pat dry. Separate into adult and children's portions. Season with salt, pepper, garlic powder, and onion powder, leaving out any seasonings that the children dislike.

Grind the mustard and fennel seeds in a spice grinder or a mortar and pestle, or place in a heavy-duty plastic bag and crush with a mallet. Mix the mustard, fennel, dried orange peel, and red pepper flakes together and press onto the adult servings.

Heat a large stovetop grill or skillet for 2 minutes over medium-high heat. Grill the halibut for 5 minutes on each side or until cooked through.

While the halibut is grilling, combine the mayonnaise, pickle relish, and celery salt in a small bowl to make the tartar sauce.

Serve the Mediterranean Grilled Halibut garnished with parsley and lemon. Serve the Simply Grilled Halibut with the tartar sauce on the side.

GROWN-UPS
Calories 200; Calories from fat 45
Total fat 4.5 g; Saturated fat 1 g
Cholesterol 55 mg; Sodium 95 mg
Carbohydrate 2 g; Dietary fiber 1 g
Sugars 1 g; Protein 36 g

CHILDREN
Calories 170; Calories from fat 35
Total fat 4 g; Saturated fat 1.5 g
Cholesterol 45 mg; Sodium 440 mg
Carbohydrate 5 g; Dietary fiber 0 g
Sugars 3 g; Protein 24 g

LEMON THYME PACIFIC COD
··
& LEMON BUTTER PACIFIC COD
··

Time to table: 15–20 minutes   Serves 2 adults and 2 or 3 children

Here cod is quickly pan-fried. For the children, the flavors come from a touch of garlic and lemon. A sweet buttery sauce finishes their variation. For the grown-ups, lemon, garlic, and fresh thyme flavor the cod. This entrée goes well with Saffron Garlic Orzo Risotto, Rotini With Roasted Red Peppers, and Italian Herbed Broiled Tomatoes.

2 Pacific cod fillets, about 1½
  pounds
4 garlic cloves, minced
2 teaspoons freshly grated lemon
  zest
Lemon wedges for garnish

GROWN-UPS
Salt and freshly ground black
  pepper to taste

1–2 tablespoons chopped fresh
  thyme or 1 tablespoon dried

CHILDREN
Salt to taste
1 tablespoon butter
2 teaspoons lemonade concentrate

Rinse the cod under cold water and pat dry. Remove any visible bones. Season the cod for the grown-ups with salt and pepper. Season the cod for the children with salt, if desired. Combine the garlic and lemon zest. Lightly season the children's portion with about a third of the mixture.

Add the thyme to the garlic-lemon mixture and spread onto the adults' portions.

Heat a nonstick skillet for 2 minutes over medium-high heat. Pan-fry the cod for 5–6 minutes on each side or until cooked through. Remove from the skillet and transfer to individual serving plates. Add the butter and lemonade to the pan. Swirl until the butter is melted. Pour the sauce over the children's servings.

GROWN-UPS
Calories 150; Calories from fat 10
Total fat 1 g; Saturated fat 0 g
Cholesterol 65 mg; Sodium 120 mg
Carbohydrate 1 g; Dietary fiber 0 g
Sugars 0 g; Protein 31 g

CHILDREN
Calories 140; Calories from fat 40
Total fat 4.5 g; Saturated fat 2.5 g
Cholesterol 50 mg; Sodium 80 mg
Carbohydrate 3 g; Dietary fiber 0 g
Sugars 2 g; Protein 20 g

BAYOU BAKED FISH

& CRISP BAKED FISH

Time to table: 25–30 minutes   Serves 2 adults and 2 or 3 children

Use any firm white fish like halibut, snapper, or cod. For the children the fish is coated with ketchup then rolled in cornflake crumbs. For the grown-ups, a sweet and savory mustard blend coats the fish before it is rolled in crumbs. The fish is oven-baked until crisp and tender. This goes well with Green Chile Rice, Cilantro Pesto Corn on the Cob, and Lemon Parsley Peas.

❝I made this when my grandchildren were over for dinner. Both adult and children's versions tasted good.❞

Olive oil cooking spray
3 cups cornflakes
2 halibut, cod, or snapper fillets
   without skin, about 1½ pounds

1 teaspoon garlic powder
1 teaspoon dried thyme
¼ teaspoon freshly ground black
   pepper

GROWN-UPS
Salt and pepper to taste
2 tablespoons honey Dijon mustard
1 teaspoon sweet paprika
¼–½ teaspoon hot paprika or
   cayenne

CHILDREN
Salt to taste
2 tablespoons ketchup

Preheat oven to 425 degrees F. Lightly spray a baking sheet with cooking spray.

Place the cornflakes in a sealable plastic bag. Squeeze out excess air and seal. Crush the cornflakes fine with a rolling pin and transfer to a pie pan. Rinse the fish under cold water and pat dry. With tweezers, remove any bones. Season the fish for the grown-ups with salt and pepper. Season the children's portions with salt. Cut the children's portions into nuggets or strips, if desired.

Place the nuggets or strips into a bowl, add the ketchup, and mix to combine. Roll the pieces in cornflakes until coated. Transfer to the prepared baking sheet and lightly coat the top with cooking spray.

Combine the honey mustard, paprikas, garlic, thyme, and pepper in a small bowl. Spread the mixture on one side of the fish meant for the adults. Place the fish, coated side down, in cornflakes and spread the mixture on the sides and top. Roll in the cornflakes until coated. Transfer to the prepared baking sheet and lightly coat the top with cooking spray.

Bake the nuggets for 10–15 minutes and the fillets for 15–20 minutes, or until done. Do not overcook. The center should no longer be translucent and the fish should flake easily with a fork.

GROWN-UPS	CHILDREN
Calories 230; Calories from fat 15	Calories 130; Calories from fat 5
Total fat 2 g; Saturated fat 0 g	Total fat 1 g; Saturated fat 0 g
Cholesterol 65 mg; Sodium 440 mg	Cholesterol 40 mg; Sodium 290 mg
Carbohydrate 22 g; Dietary fiber 0 g	Carbohydrate 10 g; Dietary fiber 0 g
Sugars 9 g; Protein 32 g	Sugars 2 g; Protein 21 g

GRILLED SHRIMP WITH THAI DIPPING SAUCE & GRILLED SHRIMP WITH COCKTAIL SAUCE

Time to table: 20–25 minutes   Serves 2 adults and 2 children

This is a very simple recipe that packs a lot of flavor. Buy the shrimp already peeled and deveined to save time. Grill the shrimp on a charcoal grill in the summer to get a more authentic flavor or broil indoors when outdoor cooking is not practical. This entrée goes well with Sesame Oriental Rice, Orange Ginger Snowpeas, and Teriyaki Sesame Broccoli.

❝I love the dipping sauce; it had a nice kick— really delicious!❞

20–25 large shrimp, peeled and deveined, about 1¼ pounds	Thai Dipping Sauce (recipe follows)
GROWN-UPS	CHILDREN
1 teaspoon red chili sauce or chili oil	½ teaspoon lemon juice
2 garlic cloves, minced	1 garlic clove, minced
1 tablespoon light teriyaki marinade	¼ cup cocktail sauce or ketchup

Start the coals or set oven controls to broil. Divide the shrimp in half and place in two separate bowls.

Add the red chili sauce, garlic, and teriyaki marinade to the shrimp for the adults. Stir to combine.

Add the lemon juice and garlic to the shrimp for the children. Stir to combine.

Skewer the shrimp using metal skewers, piercing both ends of the shrimp so that they lie flat.

Grill the shrimp over hot coals or broil for about 2 minutes per side. The shrimp will turn pink and will no longer be translucent in the center.

Serve the shrimp for the children with cocktail sauce. Serve the shrimp for the grown-ups with the Thai Dipping Sauce.

THAI DIPPING SAUCE

¼ cup rice vinegar
1 tablespoon minced fresh mint
1 tablespoon minced fresh
   cilantro

1 teaspoon fresh lime or lemon
   juice
1 teaspoon honey
⅛ teaspoon cayenne pepper

Mix together the rice vinegar, mint, cilantro, lime juice, honey, and cayenne in a small bowl.

GROWN-UPS
Calories 170; Calories from fat 15
Total fat 1.5 g; Saturated fat 0 g
Cholesterol 240 mg; Sodium 420 mg
Carbohydrate 11 g; Dietary fiber 0 g
Sugars 9 g; Protein 26 g

CHILDREN
Calories 160; Calories from fat 15
Total fat 0 g; Saturated fat 0 g
Cholesterol 240 mg; Sodium 340 mg
Carbohydrate 7 g; Dietary fiber 0 g
Sugars 6 g; Protein 27 g

SHRIMP PICCATA
& SHRIMP PARMESAN

Time to table: 15–20 minutes   Serves 2 adults and 2 children

This classic Italian dish is typically made with veal and smothered in a rich buttery sauce in which capers play the starring role. In my interpretation, succulent shrimp replace veal. The resulting dish is ready in a matter of minutes. For the children the piquant caper sauce is replaced with a light sprinkle of Parmesan cheese. This entrée goes well with Wild Mushroom Herbed Quinoa, Lemon Parsley Couscous, or Rosemary Roasted New Potatoes.

Great flavors and easy to make. Shrimp is about the only fish that my kids will eat. They loved it.

½ tablespoon butter
4 garlic cloves, sliced thin
20–25 large shrimp, peeled and
    deveined, about 1¼ pounds
2–3 tablespoons fresh lemon juice

GROWN-UPS
2 tablespoon capers, well rinsed
    and drained
Salt and pepper to taste

2 tablespoons chopped flat-leaf
    parsley

CHILDREN
2 tablespoons grated Parmesan
    cheese
Salt to taste
1 tablespoon chopped flat-leaf
    parsley (optional)

Melt the butter in a large skillet over medium-high heat. Add the garlic and shrimp. Stir until the shrimp turn pink and are no longer translucent, about 2–3 minutes. Add the lemon juice and stir to blend. Transfer the children's portion to individual dinner plates or a serving dish.

Add the capers to the skillet and stir until blended. Season with salt and pepper. Fold in the parsley and serve. Sprinkle the children's shrimp with Parmesan cheese. Season with salt. Top with parsley, if desired.

GROWN-UPS
Calories 140; Calories from fat 25
Total fat 3 g; Saturated fat 1 g
Cholesterol 245 mg; Sodium 600 mg
Carbohydrate 2 g; Dietary fiber 0 g
Sugars 1 g; Protein 26 g

CHILDREN
Calories 170; Calories from fat 40
Total fat 4.5 g; Saturated fat 2.5 g
Cholesterol 250 mg; Sodium 400 mg
Carbohydrate 2 g; Dietary fiber 0 g
Sugars 1 g; Protein 29 g

Veal Piccata: Substitute pounded veal cutlets for the shrimp. Season the cutlets with salt and pepper and dredge in flour. Saute the garlic in butter, then pan-fry the cutlets until brown on both sides. Add the lemon and proceed with instructions for both variations.

Turkey or Chicken Piccata: Substitute thin turkey cutlets for the shrimp. Follow the instructions for Veal Piccata.

LIME SKEWERED SHRIMP
& LEMON TERIYAKI SHRIMP

Time to table: 25 minutes   Serves 2 adults and 2 children

Fresh shrimp are marinated in a mixture of lime juice, soy sauce, and garlic, then skewered with lime slices. As the shrimp cook, the flavor of the lime becomes more pronounced. The shrimp are wonderful grilled over hot coals. The smoky flavor adds a nice touch. When outdoor grilling is inconvenient, use a stovetop grill pan or broiler. This goes well with Lemon Parsley Couscous, Lime Cilantro Pilaf, or Teriyaki Sesame Broccoli.

20–25 large shrimp, peeled and
   deveined, about 1¼ pounds

GROWN-UPS
¼ cup fresh lime juice
1 teaspoon dark sesame oil
2 tablespoons light soy sauce
1 medium garlic clove, minced

2 limes, scrubbed and sliced thin

CHILDREN
1–2 tablespoons lemon or lime
   juice
2 tablespoons light teriyaki
   marinade

❝*Good flavor. The kids liked both variations.*❞

Prepare the coals of an outdoor grill or set oven controls to broil.

Combine the lime juice, sesame oil, soy sauce, and garlic in a bowl. Add the shrimp for the grown-ups and marinate for 5–10 minutes. Thread the shrimp alternating with lime slices on two skewers

Combine the lemon juice and teriyaki marinade. Add the shrimp for the children and marinate for 5–10 minutes. Thread the shrimp on two skewers.

Grill or broil the skewers for about 3 minutes per side until the shrimp are no longer translucent in the center.

GROWN-UPS

Calories 150; Calories from fat 35
Total fat 3.5 g; Saturated fat 0.5 g
Cholesterol 240 mg; Sodium 380 mg
Carbohydrate 3 g; Dietary fiber 0 g
Sugars 1 g; Protein 27 g

CHILDREN

Calories 130; Calories from fat 10
Total fat 1.5 g; Saturated fat 0 g
Cholesterol 240 mg; Sodium 320 mg
Carbohydrate 3 g; Dietary fiber 0 g
Sugars 1 g; Protein 27 g

Lime Skewered Scallops: Replace the shrimp with scallops.
Lime Skewered Chicken: Replace the shrimp with boneless and skinless chicken cut into bite-size nuggets.

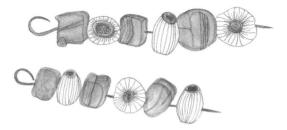

CRAB CAKES WITH ROASTED RED
....
PEPPER RELISH & CRAB CAKES
....
WITH TARTAR SAUCE
....

Time to table: 25–30 minutes   Serves 2 adults and 2 children

C rab cakes make a delightful dinner entrée, brunch, or even appetizer when made into bite-size cakes. Fresh crabmeat is mixed with egg, fresh bread crumbs, and seasonings. The cakes are formed by rolling a serving-size piece into a ball then flattening it with the hands, much like hamburger patties. Once pan-fried, they can be served with a relish or sauce. For the children, the cakes can be served in a bun, hamburger style, with tartar sauce instead of ketchup. Make tiny cakes for appetizers. This entrée goes well with Raspberry Walnut Carrot Salad or Cajun Fried Zucchini.

**❝I made tiny crab cakes for the kids,
which they liked.❞**

½ pound fresh crabmeat or canned
  lump crabmeat
2 tablespoons light mayonnaise
1 egg, lightly beaten
2 tablespoons minced onion
2 tablespoons minced celery
2 teaspoons Dijon mustard
1–2 slices soft white bread
Salt and pepper to taste
Vegetable cooking spray

GROWN-UPS
¼ cup red bell pepper, diced fine
1 teaspoon Old Bay Seasoning
Roasted Red Pepper Relish
  (recipe follows)

CHILDREN
4 tablespoons cocktail sauce
  or tartar sauce

    Carefully pick over the crabmeat, discarding any bits of shell or cartilage. In a medium-size bowl, mix together the crab, mayonnaise, egg, onion, celery, and mustard. Using a food processor, process the bread into fine crumbs. Add ½ cup bread crumbs to the crab mixture and combine well. Add more crumbs as needed until the mixture holds its shape when formed into cakes. Make two crab cakes for the children and set aside.

To the remaining mixture, stir in the diced red peppers and Old Bay Seasoning. Shape into two cakes.

Coat a nonstick skillet or griddle with vegetable cooking spray and heat over medium-high heat for 2 minutes. Pan-fry the cakes for 4–5 minutes on each side; or bake the cakes at 425 degrees F. for 20 minutes on a nonstick baking sheet.

Serve the children's crab cakes with tartar sauce and the grown-ups' crab cakes with the Roasted Red Pepper Relish.

ROASTED RED PEPPER RELISH

1 7¼-ounce jar roasted red
   peppers, rinsed and drained
1 tablespoon rice vinegar
1 garlic clove, minced

1 green onion, sliced fine
1 tablespoon honey
Salt and pepper to taste

Coarsely chop the roasted red peppers and transfer to a small bowl. Add the rice vinegar, garlic, onion, and honey. Season with salt and pepper.

GROWN-UPS
Calories 190; Calories from fat 25
Total fat 2.5 g; Saturated fat 0.5 g
Cholesterol 35 mg; Sodium 850 mg
Carbohydrate 27 g; Dietary fiber 2 g
Sugars 14 g; Protein 13 g

CHILDREN
Calories 140; Calories from fat 20
Total fat 2 g; Saturated fat 0.5 g
Cholesterol 35 mg; Sodium 730 mg
Carbohydrate 15 g; Dietary fiber 0 g
Sugars 6 g; Protein 12 g

Dill Crab Cakes: Substitute 1 tablespoon of chopped fresh dill for the Old Bay Seasoning. Serve with Dill Hollandaise Sauce (page 56) instead of Roasted Red Pepper Relish.

MEAT

....

Meat consumption has dropped significantly over the last decade as people have become more diet and fitness conscious. Although higher in fat and cholesterol than chicken or fish, meat has a place in a well-balanced diet. The leanest cuts of beef are top round, eye of round, round tip, sirloin, flank, and tenderloin. Because these cuts are lower in fat, they tend to toughen when overcooked. Use ground sirloin instead of regular ground beef, which has three times more fat. The leanest cuts of pork are the center-cut ham, loin chops, and pork tenderloin. Most cuts of veal are very lean. The leanest cuts of lamb are leg of lamb, leg chop or lamb steak, and sirloin chop.

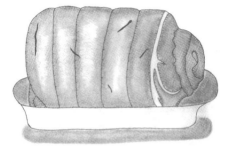

CURRIED STEAK WITH ORANGE SAUCE & ORANGE GINGER STEAK SKEWERS

Time to table: 20–25 minutes   **Serves 2 adults and 2 or 3 children**

In this recipe, a portion of the steak is cut into thin strips, skewered, and seasoned (or not) to the children's liking. The remaining portion of the steak is left whole and seasoned with a spicy rub of orange, curry, and ginger. The pan juices are deglazed with rice vinegar and orange juice concentrate to make a deliciously sweet-and-sour orange curry sauce. This goes well with Lime Cilantro Pilaf, Cilantro Quinoa Pilaf, and Garlic Roasted Asparagus or Broccoli.

❝The kids liked their portions on skewers but wanted to try the adult variation too. This meal is inexpensive and quick—a great family meal.❞

1½ pounds 1-inch-thick London
  broil, trimmed of visible fat
2 teaspoons dried orange peel or
  1½ teaspoons freshly grated
  orange zest
1 teaspoon ground ginger
½ teaspoon salt
¼ teaspoon ground white pepper

GROWN-UPS
½ teaspoon ground cumin
2 teaspoons curry powder
¼ cup rice vinegar
2 tablespoons orange juice
  concentrate

Cut about ½ pound of the steak across the grain into strips for the children. Thread the strips onto skewers.

Mix together the orange peel, ginger, salt, and white pepper. Season the skewers with a little of the mixture, if desired, or any combination that suits the children's taste.

Add the cumin and curry powder to the remaining mixture and rub onto the surface of the steak. Pan-fry the skewers for 3–4 minutes on each side, until cooked through. Remove from the pan and keep warm. Pan-fry the steak for 6–7 minutes on each side for rare or 8–9 minutes per side for medium to well done. Remove the steak from the pan.

Deglaze the pan with the vinegar and orange juice concentrate. Cook for about 1–2 minutes, scraping the bottom of the pan. Cut the steak into thin slices diagonally across the grain. Pour the sauce over the slices to serve.

GROWN-UPS
Calories 420; Calories from fat 160
Total fat 18 g; Saturated fat 8 g
Cholesterol 115 mg; Sodium 510 mg
Carbohydrate 15 g; Dietary fiber 1 g
Sugars 13 g; Protein 47 g

CHILDREN
Calories 240; Calories from fat 100
Total fat 11 g; Saturated fat 5 g
Cholesterol 75 mg; Sodium 290 mg
Carbohydrate 0 g; Dietary fiber 0 g
Sugars 0 g; Protein 31 g

GREEN PEPPERCORN STEAK
& SAVORY STEAK SKEWERS

Time to table: 20–25 minutes   **Serves 2 adults and 2 or 3 children**

For the children, a portion of the steak is cut into thin strips, skewered, and seasoned with a little garlic, onion, and thyme. For the grown-ups, the steak is left whole and further seasoned with a lively mixture of crushed green peppercorns, paprika, and coriander. The steaks can be broiled as in the instructions, pan-fried, or grilled over hot coals in the summer. This entrée goes well with Garlic Mashed Potatoes, Rotini With Roasted Red Peppers, or Garlic Roasted Broccoli.

"It sure smelled good while cooking."

1½ pounds 1-inch-thick London
   broil, trimmed of visible fat
½ teaspoon dried thyme
¼ teaspoon of each: salt, garlic
   powder, and onion powder

GROWN-UPS
1 teaspoon ground coriander
1½ teaspoons sweet paprika
1 tablespoon green peppercorns,
   drained and crushed (see note)

Light the fire of an outdoor grill or set oven controls to broil. Line a broiling pan with aluminum foil and set aside.

Cut about ½ pound of steak diagonally across the grain into thin strips. Thread the strips onto skewers. Combine the thyme, garlic, onion, and salt in a small bowl. Lightly season the skewered steak with about a third of the mixture, if acceptable to kids' taste.

Add the coriander, paprika, and peppercorns to the remaining seasoning mix. Rub the mixture on both sides of the steak.

Grill or broil the steaks for 6–7 minutes on each side for medium rare or 8–9 minutes for medium to well done. Broil the steak skewers for 3–4 minutes on each side, or until well done. Cut the steak into thin diagonal slices across the grain to serve.

Note: To crush the peppercorns, place them in a plastic bag. Squeeze out excess air and seal the bag. Place the bag on a cutting board and hit it with the flat side of a meat tenderizer until the peppercorns are thoroughly crushed.

GROWN-UPS
Calories 370; Calories from fat 160
Total fat 18 g; Saturated fat 8 g
Cholesterol 115 mg; Sodium 490 mg
Carbohydrate 3 g; Dietary fiber 1 g
Sugars 1 g; Protein 47 g

CHILDREN
Calories 240; Calories from fat 100
Total fat 11 g; Saturated fat 5 g
Cholesterol 75 mg; Sodium 190 mg
Carbohydrate 1 g; Dietary fiber 0 g
Sugars 0 g; Protein 31 g

BLEU CHEESE STEAK &
PHILADELPHIA CHEESE STEAK
SANDWICHES

Time to table: 20 minutes   Serves 2 adults and 2 children

For the grown-ups, beef tenderloin is lightly seasoned, then pan-fried. The pan juices are deglazed with balsamic vinegar and slightly thickened with bleu cheese. The intensely flavored sauce is poured over the steak or pooled onto the plate with the steak served on top. For the children, steak is cut into strips and then pan-fried. American cheese is added to the pan and stirred until just melted. More often than not, my children take just a few bites of steak, and since tenderloin is one of the most expensive cuts, I often substitute ground beef patties or a less expensive cut of meat.

Filet mignon steaks are generally cut from 1 to 1½ inches thick, which can take longer to cook. I prefer to use a thinner cut, about ½ inch thick, to keep portion size to a reasonable 4–6 ounces and also to speed up the cooking time.

This entrée goes well with Rosemary Roasted New Potatoes, Garlic Roasted Asparagus or Broccoli, and Italian Herbed Broiled Tomatoes.

2 filet mignon steaks, about ¾
pound each
¼ teaspoon of each: salt, pepper,
onion powder, and garlic powder
1 teaspoon dried thyme

GROWN-UPS
¼ cup balsamic vinegar

2 tablespoons crumbled bleu cheese

CHILDREN
2 slices American or Swiss cheese
cut into 4 or 5 strips
2 French rolls or hamburger buns

❝*Excellent. Will do it again—especially the sauce. The children liked the steak on rolls. One had the steak with cheese and the other without. Easy to make both.*❞

Trim the steaks of visible fat. If the steaks are cut thick, slice them in half so that they are only ½ inch thick, or have the butcher do this for you. Slice the children's portion into thin strips. Season the steak and strips with salt, pepper, onion powder, garlic powder, and thyme, omitting any that the children dislike.

Heat a nonstick skillet over medium-high heat for 2 minutes. Pan-fry the strips for the children for 4–6 minutes, until well done. Add the cheese and stir until melted, about 30 seconds. Arrange the meat on the French rolls and keep warm in the oven until ready to serve.

Wipe out the skillet with paper towels. Pan-fry the steaks for 3–4 minutes on each side for medium rare or 6–7 minutes for well done. Transfer the steaks to individual plates. Pour the balsamic vinegar into the skillet. Scrape the bottom of the pan to loosen bits of brown meat and seasonings. Add the bleu cheese and stir until melted. Do not allow the sauce to cool. Pool the sauce on the plate with the steak placed on top, or pour the sauce over the steak. Serve immediately.

GROWN-UPS
Calories 410; Calories from fat 180
Total fat 20 g; Saturated fat 9 g
Cholesterol 150 mg; Sodium 230 mg
Carbohydrate 5 g; Dietary fiber 0 g
Sugars 5 g; Protein 50 g

CHILDREN
Calories 400; Calories from fat 160
Total fat 17 g; Saturated fat 8 g
Cholesterol 110 mg; Sodium 500 mg
Carbohydrate 19 g; Dietary fiber 1 g
Sugars 1 g; Protein 38 g

STEAK WITH MADEIRA MUSHROOM
SAUCE & STEAK KABOBS

Time to table: 25–30 minutes   Serves 2 adults and 2 or 3 children

For the children, a portion of the steak is cut into chunks, then skewered to make kabobs. The adult portion is left whole, then pan-fried, sliced across the grain, and smothered in a tasty mushroom sauce. The kabobs give children their own personalized serving. When making kabobs, I often carry the theme to other parts of the meal, time permitting. Skewer small new potatoes and roast in the oven. Skewer cherry tomatoes, cucumber wedges, and celery instead of salad, and serve the dressing on the side. This entrée goes well with Garlic Mashed Potatoes, Thyme Roasted Carrots, or Garlic Roasted Broccoli.

❝The sauce was wonderful. I made the variation with dried porcini mushrooms. The sauce had an intense earthy and smoky flavor. Just delicious.❞

1¼ pounds London broil
¼ teaspoon onion powder
¼ teaspoon garlic powder
½ teaspoon dried thyme
Salt and pepper to taste

GROWN-UPS
½ pound fresh mushrooms, cleaned
  and sliced
½ teaspoon dried thyme
¼ cup Madeira
¼ cup beef broth

Trim the steak of visible fat. Cut about ½ pound of steak into chunks for the children, leaving the rest of the steak in one piece. Season the chunks and the steak with onion powder, garlic powder, thyme, salt, and pepper, omitting any seasonings that the children dislike. Thread the chunks on 6-inch skewers.

Heat a large nonstick skillet over medium-high heat for 2 minutes. Pan-fry the steak for 7–8 minutes on each side for medium rare, and the kabobs for 4–5 minutes on each side, until well done. Transfer the steak and kabobs to a platter and keep warm until ready to serve.

Add the mushrooms and thyme to the skillet. Sauté over medium to high heat until the mushrooms are browned, 3–4 minutes. Pour the Madeira and beef broth into the pan, scraping up bits of meat and seasonings stuck to the bottom. Bring the mixture to a boil and let it reduce by half, about 5 minutes. Season with salt and pepper.

To serve, cut the steak into thin slices diagonally across the grain. Spoon the mushroom sauce over the sliced steak. Place the kabobs on individual plates for the children.

GROWN-UPS

Calories 430; Calories from fat 160
Total fat 18 g; Saturated fat 8 g
Cholesterol 115 mg; Sodium 160 mg
Carbohydrate 9 g; Dietary fiber 2 g
Sugars 5 g; Protein 49 g

CHILDREN

Calories 240; Calories from fat 100
Total fat 11 g; Saturated fat 5 g
Cholesterol 75 mg; Sodium 95 mg
Carbohydrate 0 g; Dietary fiber 0 g
Sugars 0 g; Protein 31 g

Madeira and Porcini Mushroom Sauce: Use 1/2 ounce of dried porcini mushrooms. At the start of the recipe, place the porcini, Madeira, and beef broth in a microwave-safe dish. Cover and microwave at full power for about 5 minutes. Let stand until ready to use.

Follow the recipe instructions above. After adding the fresh mushrooms and thyme to the skillet, remove the porcini mushrooms from the soaking liquid. Rinse under cold water to remove any residual sand and chop. Add the porcini to the skillet. Line a strainer with a coffee filter and pour the mushroom soaking liquid through it into the skillet.

ROSEMARY DIJON PORK CHOPS
& PEACHY KEEN PORK CHOPS

Time to table: 20–25 minutes   Serves 2 adults and 2 or 3 children

Center-cut pork chops are lightly seasoned then pan-fried. For the children, the chops are glazed with peach or apricot preserves. For the grown-ups, a rich-tasting sauce made with honey Dijon mustard, balsamic vinegar, and rosemary dresses up the chops. Use thin-cut pork chops for this recipe. The chops have to cook quickly before the pan juices scorch, giving the sauce a bitter flavor. This recipe goes well with Lemon Parsley Peas, Dilly Green Beans, and Garlic Roasted Broccoli.

> ❝The flavors in the sauce were a wonderful combination of sweet and savory. My husband doesn't usually like vinegar and Dijon mustard, but he really liked this sauce. He said the rosemary was a strong enough flavor to carry the sauce. The kids said that the peach preserves were great on the chops.❞

4–6 center-cut pork chops, thin cut
¼ teaspoon of each: salt, pepper,
　garlic powder, and onion powder

GROWN-UPS
Rosemary Mustard Sauce
　(recipe follows)

CHILDREN
1–2 tablespoons peach or apricot
　preserves

Trim the pork chops of visible fat. Season with salt, pepper, garlic powder, and onion powder, omitting any that the children dislike. Heat a large nonstick skillet over medium-high heat for 2 minutes. Pan-fry the chops for 4–5 minutes on each side or until cooked through. Transfer the chops to a plate and keep warm until ready to serve.

To serve, glaze the chops for the children with the peach preserves. Pour the mustard sauce over the chops for the grown-ups.

ROSEMARY MUSTARD SAUCE

1 teaspoon olive oil
2 garlic cloves, minced
½ tablespoon chopped fresh
　rosemary
½ cup minced shallots
3 tablespoons honey Dijon mustard

2 tablespoons balsamic vinegar
½ cup low-sodium, fat-free chicken
　broth
Salt and freshly ground pepper
　to taste
1–2 teaspoons honey (optional)

Heat the same skillet that the chops were cooked in over medium-high heat. Pour the oil into the center of the skillet. Add the garlic and rosemary. Stir for 1 minute. Add the shallots and stir until soft, about 3–5 minutes. Add a teaspoon of water if the skillet is too dry. Stir in the mustard, balsamic vinegar, and broth. Bring to a boil and let the mixture reduce and thicken, about 5–7 minutes. Season with salt and pepper. Taste and add the honey to balance the flavors, if needed.

GROWN-UPS
Calories 250; Calories from fat 80
Total fat 9 g; Saturated fat 2 g
Cholesterol 60 mg; Sodium 480 mg
Carbohydrate 16 g; Dietary fiber 0 g
Sugars 6 g; Protein 26 g

CHILDREN
Calories 120; Calories from fat 30
Total fat 3.5 g; Saturated fat 1 g
Cholesterol 40 mg; Sodium 50 mg
Carbohydrate 9 g; Dietary fiber 0 g
Sugars 5 g; Protein 14 g

PORK MEDALLIONS WITH GARLIC
GINGER PLUM SAUCE &
PORK MEDALLIONS WITH
SWEET PLUM SAUCE

Time to table: 20–25 minutes   Serves 2 adults and 2 or 3 children

Pork tenderloin is sliced into thin medallions, then quickly pan-seared. Plum jam and balsamic vinegar form the base of this sweet garlicky and gingery sauce. For the children, simple plum jam accompanies the pork, or substitute applesauce if more to their liking. This recipe goes well with Teriyaki Sesame Broccoli, Lime Cilantro Pilaf, Sesame Oriental Rice, or Orange Ginger Glazed Carrots.

❝This is a really fast and tasty dish. We love the sauce.❞

1 small pork tenderloin, trimmed
   of visible fat, about 1½ pounds
¼ teaspoon of each: salt, pepper,
   and garlic powder

GROWN-UPS
Garlic Ginger Plum Sauce
   (recipe follows)

CHILDREN
2 tablespoons plum jam
   or applesauce

Slice the pork tenderloin into medallions about 1/2 inch thick. Season with salt, pepper, and garlic powder, omitting any that the children dislike. Heat a large nonstick skillet over medium-high heat for 2 minutes. Place the medallions in the skillet so that they do not overlap. Cook for 3–4 minutes on each side or until cooked through. Remove from the skillet and keep warm in the oven until ready to serve.

For the children, serve the pork with plum jam on the side. For the grown-ups, serve the pork with the Garlic Ginger Plum Sauce spooned over the top.

GARLIC GINGER PLUM SAUCE

1 teaspoon olive oil
1 teaspoon grated fresh ginger
2 garlic cloves, minced

2 tablespoons plum jam
½ tablespoon balsamic vinegar

Wipe the skillet with paper towels. Pour the olive oil into the center of the skillet and heat for 2 minutes over medium-high heat. Add the ginger and garlic to the oil. Stir for 2–3 minutes until fragrant. Add the plum jam and balsamic vinegar. Heat through and serve.

GROWN-UPS
Calories 270; Calories from fat 50
Total fat 6 g; Saturated fat 2 g
Cholesterol 110 mg; Sodium 95 mg
Carbohydrate 15 g; Dietary fiber 0 g
Sugars 9 g; Protein 36 g

CHILDREN
Calories 180; Calories from fat 35
Total fat 4 g; Saturated fat 1.5 g
Cholesterol 75 mg; Sodium 65 mg
Carbohydrate 0 g; Dietary fiber 0 g
Sugars 5 g; Protein 24 g

PORK CHOPS WITH SPICY APPLE CHUTNEY & PORK CHOPS WITH SWEET APPLE CHUTNEY

Time to table: 25–30 minutes   Serves 2 adults and 2 or 3 children

Here pork chops are lightly seasoned, then rubbed with dried sage. The fresh apple chutney is spiced with cinnamon, ginger, cloves, and cardamom for a slightly exotic twist. Red onions, garlic, and pickled jalapeño peppers add a savory and piquant punch. The children will enjoy a more mildly flavored variation of the chutney, or serve applesauce instead if more to their liking. Begin the chutney at the start of the recipe since it takes longer to cook than the pork. This entrée goes well with Garlic Mashed Potatoes, Lemon Parsley Couscous, Orange Ginger Asparagus, and Garlic Roasted Broccoli.

4 center-cut pork chops, trimmed
   of visible fat
¼ teaspoon each: salt, pepper,
   onion powder, and garlic powder
Apple Chutney (recipe follows)

GROWN-UPS
½ teaspoon rubbed sage or poultry
   seasoning

❝My family really enjoyed this. It was a nice change from the usual thing. I liked starting with a real apple—felt very healthy.❞

Preheat broiler. Line a broiling pan with aluminum foil and set aside. Season the chops with salt, pepper, garlic powder, and onion powder, omitting any that the children dislike. Season the pork chops for the grown-ups with sage. Broil the chops for 5–6 minutes on each side until cooked through. Serve with the Apple Chutney on the side.

APPLE CHUTNEY

1 large Golden Delicious apple, cored and chopped, about 1½ cups
2 tablespoons raisins or dried cranberries
3 tablespoons apple cider vinegar
2 tablespoons brown sugar
½ teaspoon ground ginger

¼ teaspoon ground cinnamon
⅛ teaspoon ground cloves
⅛ teaspoon ground cardamom

GROWN-UPS
¼ cup chopped red onion
2 garlic cloves, minced
1–2 teaspoons chopped jalapeño peppers, canned or jarred

Heat a large nonstick skillet for 2 minutes over medium-high heat. Add apples and raisins. Stir for 3–4 minutes, or until soft. Add the cider vinegar, brown sugar, ginger, cinnamon, cloves, and cardamom. Cover, reduce heat, and simmer for 5 minutes. Remove half of the mixture for the children and transfer to a small bowl.

To the remaining mixture, add the onion, garlic, and jalapeño peppers. Cover and simmer for 10 minutes.

GROWN-UPS
Calories 220; Calories from fat 60
Total fat 7 g; Saturated fat 2.5 g
Cholesterol 60 mg; Sodium 75 mg
Carbohydrate 19 g; Dietary fiber 2 g
Sugars 17 g; Protein 20 g

CHILDREN
Calories 140; Calories from fat 40
Total fat 4.5 g; Saturated fat 1.5 g
Cholesterol 40 mg; Sodium 40 mg
Carbohydrate 11 g; Dietary fiber 0 g
Sugars 10 g; Protein 13 g

PORK WITH BURGUNDY CRANBERRY
SAUCE & PORK WITH SPICED
CRANBERRY SAUCE

Time to table: 20–25 minutes   Serves 2 adults and 2 or 3 children

This quick weeknight meal can be made year-round since dried cranberries are always in season. The sweet and tart sauce is created by simmering cranberries, ginger, currant jelly, balsamic vinegar, and orange juice together. Once the sauce is done, a portion is removed for the children. Red wine is added to the adult portion. The sauce is reduced to concentrate and balance the hearty flavors. Prepare the cranberry sauce at the start of the recipe since it takes longer to cook than the pork. For entertaining, roast a whole pork or beef tenderloin for a more elegant meal. This entrée goes well with Garlic Mashed Potatoes, Rosemary Roasted New Potatoes, or Lemon Minted Peas.

**❝The sauce was great. Would go well with game
and poultry, too.❞**

4 center-cut pork chops   Cranberry Sauce
¼ teaspoon each: salt, pepper,   (recipe follows)
   and garlic powder

Trim the pork of visible fat and season with salt, pepper, and garlic powder, omitting any that the children find objectionable. Heat a non-stick skillet over medium-high heat for 2 minutes. Pan-fry the pork chops for 5–6 minutes on each side or until cooked through. Place on individual serving plates with the Cranberry Sauce on the side.

CRANBERRY SAUCE

1 cup dried cranberries
1 teaspoon grated fresh ginger
¼ cup red currant jelly
2 tablespoons balsamic vinegar

¼ teaspoon grated orange zest
¼ cup orange juice

GROWN-UPS
½ cup burgundy

Combine the cranberries, ginger, jelly, balsamic vinegar, orange zest, and orange juice in a saucepan. Bring to a boil, reduce heat, cover, and simmer until cranberries are soft, about 10 minutes. Separate the children's portions and transfer to a small bowl. Add the burgundy to the remaining cranberries and bring to a boil. Let the mixture reduce by half, 5–8 minutes.

GROWN-UPS
Calories 340; Calories from fat 45
Total fat 5 g; Saturated fat 1.5 g
Cholesterol 65 mg; Sodium 50 mg
Carbohydrate 38 g; Dietary fiber 7 g
Sugars 35 g; Protein 23 g

CHILDREN
Calories 200; Calories from fat 30
Total fat 3.5 g; Saturated fat 1 g
Cholesterol 45 mg; Sodium 30 mg
Carbohydrate 25 g; Dietary fiber 5 g
Sugars 23 g; Protein 15 g

Dried Cherry Sauce: Substitute dried cherries for the cranberries.

MOROCCAN SPICED LAMB
···
& ORANGE SPICED LAMB
···

Time to table: 20 minutes   **Serves 2 adults and 2 or 3 children**

Moroccan cuisine more than any other makes use of aromatic seasonings like cinnamon, cloves, and cardamom in main dishes rather than just desserts. These spices add a slightly sweet flavor that is truly enjoyable. This recipe goes well with Lemon Parsley Couscous, Lemon Minted Peas, or Orange Ginger Asparagus.

❝Very fast and easy to do. The flavor is typical of Arabic cuisine. The children's part was good and flavorful too, but not overpowering.❞

2 teaspoons dried orange peel
½ teaspoon salt
½ teaspoon garlic powder
½ teaspoon onion powder
¼ teaspoon ground white pepper
¼ teaspoon ground cinnamon
⅛ teaspoon ground cardamom
   or cloves

2 or 3 leg chops or lamb steaks,
   about 1½ pounds

GROWN-UPS
1 teaspoon ground coriander
½ teaspoon ground turmeric
½ teaspoon ground cumin
Dash of cayenne pepper

In a small bowl mix together the orange peel, salt, garlic powder, onion powder, white pepper, cinnamon, and cardamom. Lightly season the children's portions with about a third of the mixture.

To the remaining mixture add the coriander, turmeric, cumin, and cayenne. Season the grown-ups' portions.

Heat a nonstick skillet over medium-high heat for 2 minutes. Pan-fry the lamb for about 5 minutes per side or until medium rare.

GROWN-UPS
Calories 250; Calories from fat 90
Total fat 10 g; Saturated fat 4.5 g
Cholesterol 110 mg; Sodium 410 mg
Carbohydrate 2 g; Dietary fiber 0 g
Sugars 1 g; Protein 36 g

CHILDREN
Calories 170; Calories from fat 60
Total fat 7 g; Saturated fat 3 g
Cholesterol 75 mg; Sodium 270 mg
Carbohydrate 1 g; Dietary fiber 0 g
Sugars 0 g; Protein 24 g

GRILLED LAMB CHOPS WITH THAI
··
MINT SAUCE & GRILLED LAMB CHOPS
··
WITH MINT JELLY
······························

Time to table: 20–25 minutes   Serves 2 adults and 2 or 3 children

Lamb and mint are inextricably linked together. When I was a child, a jar of mint jelly was always on the table whenever lamb was served. For this recipe, I developed a more sophisticated mint sauce for the grown-ups, but for the children, old traditions are best left unchanged. This recipe goes well with Lime Cilantro Pilaf, Saffron Garlic Orzo Risotto, Cardamom Spiced Butternut Squash, and Lemon Minted Peas.

2 or 3 leg chops or lamb steaks,
about 1½ pounds
¼ teaspoon each: salt, pepper,
garlic powder, and onion powder

GROWN-UPS
Thai Mint Sauce (recipe follows)

CHILDREN
2–3 tablespoons mint jelly

Heat a stovetop grill pan for 2 minutes over medium-high heat. Season the lamb with the salt, pepper, garlic powder, and onion powder, omitting any that the children dislike. Grill for 4–5 minutes per side for medium rare or longer for well done.

For the children, serve the lamb on individual plates with the mint jelly on the side. For the grown-ups, serve the lamb on individual plates. Spoon the Thai Mint Sauce over the meat.

THAI MINT SAUCE

¼ cup rice vinegar
1½ tablespoons minced mint
½ tablespoon minced green onion

1 tablespoon fresh lime juice
1 teaspoon honey
⅓ teaspoon red pepper flakes

In a small microwave-safe dish, combine the rice vinegar, mint, green onion, lime juice, honey, and red pepper flakes. Microwave at full power for 30–45 seconds to warm.

GROWN-UPS
Calories 290; Calories from fat 90
Total fat 10 g; Saturated fat 4.5 g
Cholesterol 110 mg; Sodium 680 mg
Carbohydrate 11 g; Dietary fiber 0 g
Sugars 9 g; Protein 36 g

CHILDREN
Calories 210; Calories from fat 60
Total fat 7 g; Saturated fat 3 g
Cholesterol 75 mg; Sodium 480 mg
Carbohydrate 13 g; Dietary fiber 0 g
Sugars 13 g; Protein 24 g

VEAL SCALOPPINI & VEAL PARMESAN

Time to table: 25–30 minutes   Serves 2 adults and 2 or 3 children

Thin slices of veal are dredged in Parmesan cheese, then pan-fried. (Use the store-bought grated cheese rather than freshly grated Parmesan.) For the grown-ups, a savory mushroom sauce made with sun-dried tomatoes and Madeira completes the dish. For the children, the veal is covered with pizza sauce and mozzarella cheese. This recipe goes well with Greek Capellini, Pesto Polenta, Dilly Green Beans, and Thyme Roasted New Potatoes.

1½ pounds veal, sliced very thin
2 tablespoons Parmesan cheese

GROWN-UPS
Salt and pepper to taste
½ pound fresh mushrooms, cleaned
    and sliced
¼ cup Madeira
½ cup beef broth

2 tablespoons oil-packed sun-dried
    tomatoes, well rinsed and
    drained
2 tablespoons chopped fresh flat-
    leaf parsley

CHILDREN
Salt to taste
½ cup pizza or spaghetti sauce
¼ cup grated mozzarella cheese

❝*The sun-dried tomatoes really added zip; parsley was pretty. I love the adult/child variations.*❞

Tenderize the veal by pounding with a meat tenderizer. Season the adult portion with salt and pepper and the children's portion with salt. Dredge the veal in Parmesan cheese. Heat a large nonstick skillet for 2 minutes over high heat. Brown the veal for 2–3 minutes on both sides until cooked through. Remove from the skillet. Transfer the children's portion to a microwave-safe dish. Pour the pizza sauce over the veal and top with mozzarella cheese. Cover with vented plastic wrap and microwave at full power for 2–3 minutes, until the sauce is heated and the cheese is melted. Let stand until ready to serve.

Add the mushrooms to the skillet and stir until browned, about 3–4 minutes. Add the Madeira and beef broth, stirring to loosen bits of browned meat. Bring to a boil and let the mixture reduce by half, about 5 minutes. Add the sun-dried tomatoes and return the veal to the skillet. Heat through and stir in the parsley. Season with salt and pepper.

GROWN-UPS	CHILDREN
Calories 330; Calories from fat 100	Calories 210; Calories from fat 80
Total fat 11 g; Saturated fat 4 g	Total fat 9 g; Saturated fat 4 g
Cholesterol 115 mg; Sodium 230 mg	Cholesterol 80 mg; Sodium 300 mg
Carbohydrate 10 g; Dietary fiber 2 g	Carbohydrate 4 g; Dietary fiber 1 g
Sugars 5 g; Protein 39 g	Sugars 2 g; Protein 27 g

VEAL CUTLETS WITH FENNEL MUSTARD SAUCE & VEAL CUTLETS WITH PARMESAN

Time to table: 20–25 minutes   Serves 2 adults and 2 or 3 children

Tender veal cutlets are lightly seasoned and pan-fried. For the grown-ups, a spicy mustard sauce made with fennel and fresh dill tops the cutlets, and for the children a light sprinkle of Parmesan cheese completes the dish. This dish goes well with Garlic Mashed Potatoes, Greek-Style Green Beans, or Garlic Roasted Broccoli.

❝*Great recipe! Loved the mustard sauce.*❞

1¼ pound veal cutlets, sliced thin

GROWN-UPS
Salt and black pepper to taste
Fennel Mustard Sauce
 (recipe follows)

CHILDREN
Salt to taste
2 tablespoons grated Parmesan cheese

Heat a nonstick skillet over medium-high heat for 2 minutes. Tenderize the veal by pounding with a meat tenderizer. Season the adult portion with salt and pepper and the children's portion with salt. Place the cutlets in the skillet so that they do not overlap. Cook for 3–4 minutes per side or until no longer pink.

To serve, sprinkle Parmesan cheese over the veal for the children and spoon the mustard sauce over the adult servings.

Fennel Mustard Sauce

½ tablespoon olive oil
2 teaspoons yellow mustard seeds
2 teaspoons fennel seeds
¼ teaspoon red pepper flakes
1 teaspoon lemon zest
1 tablespoon lemon juice

2 tablespoons Dijon mustard
2 tablespoons honey
½ cup chicken broth
1½ tablespoons chopped dill
    or parsley
Salt and pepper to taste

Heat the olive oil in a small saucepan or skillet for 2–3 minutes over medium-high heat. Add the mustard and fennel seeds and stir for about 2 minutes or until the seeds begin to pop. Add the red pepper flakes, lemon zest, lemon juice, Dijon mustard, and honey. Stir to combine. Pour in the chicken broth and stir until blended. Turn heat to high and allow the mixture to reduce and thicken, about 5 minutes. Pour the sauce through a strainer into a bowl. Stir in the dill and season with salt and pepper.

GROWN-UPS
Calories 330; Calories from fat 120
Total fat 13 g; Saturated fat 3.5 g
Cholesterol 95 mg; Sodium 490 mg
Carbohydrate 22 g; Dietary fiber 2 g
Sugars 17 g; Protein 32 g

CHILDREN
Calories 140; Calories from fat 60
Total fat 6 g; Saturated fat 2.5 g
Cholesterol 65 mg; Sodium 120 mg
Carbohydrate 0 g; Dietary fiber 0 g
Sugars 0 g; Protein 20 g

POULTRY

....

P oultry is much lower in fat than most red meat, although the fat content varies considerably between light and dark meat. Light meat has less fat and tends to be drier than dark. Many children prefer dark meat over white because it is moister. Many of the recipes in this section use boneless, skinless chicken breast meat because the cooking time is so quick, just 10–20 minutes, perfect for weeknight meals. Remove the tenderloin (the strip of meat close to the bone side of the breast), and if the breast meat is particularly thick, pound it between plastic wrap at the thickest part with the flat side of a meat tenderizer. This ensures even and quick cooking.

For the children, I often use boneless thigh meat. You may substitute other pieces of poultry if the children have a preference, although the cooking times will probably be different from those in the recipes. Chicken is cooked thoroughly when the internal temperature reaches 165 degrees F. Use an instant-read thermometer inserted into the thickest part of the meat without touching bone. When cooked through, the meat is no longer translucent in the center.

For adults, who are watching their calories, portion size is 4–6 ounces of meat. Discard the skin, since it contains most of the calories from fat.

I prefer to use fresh chicken, but I don't always have time to stop off at the grocery store—so I keep a supply of boneless and skinless chicken breasts, skinless thighs, chicken tenderloins, and drumsticks in the freezer. Bought in bulk and individually frozen, it is easy to mix different pieces at the same meal. To thaw quickly, put the pieces in warm water for about 5–10 minutes.

I'm a fanatic about safe handling procedures because of the potential for salmonella contamination. At the store, place fresh poultry in plastic so the juices cannot drip on other food in the shopping cart. When ready to cook, remove the packaging and wash the chicken in the sink. Use a separate cutting board to cut it up. Once the chicken is cooking, use a disinfectant to spray down the sink, counters, and all the utensils that came into contact with the raw chicken. Wash your hands well with soap before moving on with the rest of the meal preparation.

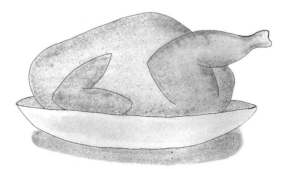

ORANGE CURRY CHICKEN
& ORANGE SESAME CHICKEN

Time to table: 20–25 minutes   Serves 2 adults and 2 to 4 children

A pungent orange curry paste seasons the chicken with intense flavor on the outside. Use boneless and skinless chicken breast or thigh meat. Remove the chicken tenderloins (thin strip of meat) from the rib side of the chicken breasts and if the chicken is particularly thick, pound it to ¼ inch thick so that it cooks quickly. Many children prefer the flavor of dark meat; use boneless chicken thighs for them, if desired. This recipe goes well with Lime Cilantro Pilaf, Cilantro Quinoa Pilaf, Cardamom Spiced Butternut Squash, or Garlic Roasted Asparagus.

❝This is a great combination of flavors. The sesame seeds toast as the chicken cooks.❞

3 or 4 boneless and skinless
  chicken breast halves
2 tablespoons sesame seeds
1 tablespoon honey
2 tablespoons orange juice
  concentrate, thawed
2 teaspoons dried orange peel or
  1½ teaspoons freshly grated
  orange zest

3 garlic cloves, minced

GROWN-UPS
Salt and pepper to taste
½ tablespoon curry powder

CHILDREN
Salt to taste

Set oven temperature to broil. Line a broiling pan with aluminum foil.

Rinse the chicken under cold water and pat dry. Season the pieces for the grown-ups with salt and pepper. Season the pieces for the children with salt. In a small bowl, combine the sesame seeds, honey, orange juice concentrate, orange peel, and garlic. Transfer half of the mixture to another dish. Stir the curry powder into the mixture.

Place the chicken, smooth side down, on the broiling pan. Spread the milder seasoning paste on the chicken for the children and the curry paste on the chicken for the grown-ups.

Broil for 5–6 minutes. Turn the chicken over and spread the paste on the other side. Broil for another 5–6 minutes, until cooked through.

GROWN-UPS
Calories 320; Calories from fat 50
Total fat 5 g; Saturated fat 1 g
Cholesterol 135 mg; Sodium 160 mg
Carbohydrate 11 g; Dietary fiber 1 g
Sugars 8 g; Protein 56 g

CHILDREN
Calories 110; Calories from fat 35
Total fat 4 g; Saturated fat 1 g
Cholesterol 55 mg; Sodium 60 mg
Carbohydrate 5 g; Dietary fiber 0 g
Sugars 4 g; Protein 14 g

CHICKEN PUTTANESCA
& ITALIAN CHICKEN

Time to table: 20 minutes   Serves 2 adults and 2 or 3 children

Puttanesca sauce is a spicy mixture of tomatoes, onions, capers, black olives, anchovies, garlic, and oregano. My adaptations starts with a full-flavored spaghetti sauce. With the many gourmet flavors now available, use one that everyone likes. The chicken is seasoned, then pan-fried. Once the children's servings are removed, the sauce takes on a new dimension with the addition of Greek olives, capers, fresh dill, and anchovies for those who like them. This entrée goes well with Polenta, Garlic Roasted Broccoli or Asparagus, and Saffron Garlic Orzo Risotto.

4 boneless and skinless chicken
    breast halves, about 1½ pounds
1 26½-ounce can pasta sauce
¼ teaspoon of each: salt, pepper,
    garlic powder, and onion powder
Grated Parmesan cheese for
    garnish

GROWN-UPS
6–8 pitted Greek olives, rinsed and
    chopped
1 tablespoon capers, rinsed and
    drained
2–3 tablespoons chopped fresh dill
1–2 teaspoons chopped anchovies
    (optional)
Pepper to taste

Heat a large nonstick skillet over medium-high heat for 2 minutes. Season the chicken with salt, pepper, garlic powder, and onion powder. Place the chicken in the skillet so that the pieces do not overlap. Cook for 4–5 minutes on each side until the chicken is cooked through.

Remove the children's portions and transfer to a microwave-safe dish. Pour half of the pasta sauce over the chicken and heat in the microwave at full power for 2–3 minutes.

Add the remaining sauce to the skillet along with the olives, capers, and dill. Spoon the sauce over the chicken and heat through. Stir in the anchovies, if using. Season with pepper.

GROWN-UPS
Calories 330; Calories from fat 40
Total fat 4.5 g; Saturated fat 1.5 g
Cholesterol 100 mg; Sodium 960 mg
Carbohydrate 25 g; Dietary fiber 4 g
Sugars 16 g; Protein 44 g

CHILDREN
Calories 190; Calories from fat 20
Total fat 2 g; Saturated fat 0.5 g
Cholesterol 70 mg; Sodium 350 mg
Carbohydrate 12 g; Dietary fiber 2 g
Sugars 8 g; Protein 30 g

CHICKEN WITH SPICY MOLE SAUCE
& CHICKEN FINGERS WITH MOLE
DIPPING SAUCE

Time to table: 25–30 minutes   Serves 2 adults and 2 to 4 children

Mole (pronounced moh-lay) is a Mexican delicacy. It comes from the word *molli*, meaning "concoction." Traditionally the sauce is a smooth blend of onions, garlic, chiles, and ground seeds with a hint of chocolate. The ingredients for mole can be many and there are as many variations of the dish as there are cooks. In my interpretation, I've simplified the ingredients, making the recipe suitable for a weeknight meal. For the children, a milder variation of the sauce (slightly sweet and chocolaty) is served on the side with chicken fingers for dipping. This recipe goes well with Lime Cilantro Pilaf, Lemon Parsley Couscous, and Sesame Oriental Rice.

❝Very unusual and rich-tasting sauce.❞

4 boneless and skinless chicken
  breast halves, about 1½
  pounds
½ medium onion, minced
2 garlic cloves, minced
1 teaspoon cinnamon
1 teaspoon chili powder
½ teaspoon cumin
1 8½-ounce can plain tomato sauce
2 tablespoons smooth peanut
  butter
2 tablespoons honey
½ tablespoon dark sesame oil

½ ounce semisweet baking
  chocolate, chopped into small
  pieces
Toasted sesame seeds for garnish
  (optional)

GROWN-UPS
Salt and pepper to taste
½ teaspoon or more red chili sauce
1 tablespoon minced jalapeño
  peppers, canned or jarred

CHILDREN
Salt to taste

Rinse the chicken and pat dry. Remove the tenderloin from the rib side of the chicken. Season the chicken for the grown-ups with salt and pepper. Season the chicken for the children with salt. Cut the children's portion into strips, leaving the adults' portion whole. Heat a large nonstick skillet over medium-high heat for 2 minutes. Place the chicken into the skillet so that the pieces do not overlap. Cook until no longer translucent in the center, 5–6 minutes on each side for the breasts and 4–5 minutes on each side for the strips. As the chicken is cooked through, transfer it to an overproof plate and keep warm in the oven.

Add the onion and garlic to the skillet. Stir until the onion is soft, about 3 minutes. Add the cinnamon, chili powder, and cumin. Stir for 1 minute to release the flavors. Add the tomato sauce, peanut butter, honey, and sesame oil. Cook over low heat for about 10 minutes. Add the chocolate and stir until melted. Transfer half of the sauce to individual bowls for the children.

Stir the red chili sauce and jalapeño peppers into the remaining sauce in the skillet.

Place the chicken for the grown-ups into the skillet. Cover with sauce and heat through, about 5 minutes. Serve garnished with sesame seeds, if desired. Serve the chicken fingers with the mole sauce on the side for dipping.

GROWN-UPS
Calories 330; Calories from fat 90
Total fat 10 g; Saturated fat 2.5 g
Cholesterol 100 mg; Sodium 550 mg
Carbohydrate 21 g; Dietary fiber 3 g
Sugars 13 g; Protein 43 g

CHILDREN
Calories 220; Calories from fat 60
Total fat 6 g; Saturated fat 1.5 g
Cholesterol 65 mg; Sodium 380 mg
Carbohydrate 13 g; Dietary fiber 2 g
Sugars 9 g; Protein 29 g

TERIYAKI HONEY GLAZED DRUMSTICKS & LEMON HONEY GLAZED DRUMSTICKS

Time to table: 30–35 minutes   Serves 2 adults (2 drumsticks each) and 2 to 4 children

This sweet-tart honey glaze goes well with just about any cut of chicken. I originally used it to glaze Cornish game hens, which are great for entertaining. For weeknight meals, drumsticks are used. For grown-ups watching their calories, chicken breast is much lower in fat. This recipe goes well with Teriyaki Sesame Broccoli or Asparagus and Sesame Oriental Rice.

❝It's a wonderful everyday recipe. My children liked both variations.❞

8 chicken drumsticks
½ cup honey
2 teaspoons grated lemon zest
2 tablespoons fresh lemon juice

GROWN-UPS
Salt and pepper to taste

1 teaspoon dark sesame oil
2 teaspoons light soy sauce

CHILDREN
Salt to taste

Preheat oven to 425 degrees F. Line the bottom and rack of a broiler pan with aluminum foil. Poke holes in the foil to allow the juices to drain while cooking.

Rinse the chicken under cold water and pat dry. Remove the skin from the grown-ups' servings, leaving the skin on the children's portions, if desired. Season the chicken for the grown-ups with salt and pepper. Season the chicken for the children with salt, if desired. Place the drumsticks on the broiler pan.

Mix the honey, lemon zest, and lemon juice together. Transfer half of the mixture to another dish. Brush on the children's servings.

Stir in the sesame oil and soy sauce to the other half of the honey mixture. Brush on the grown-ups' servings.

Bake in the oven for 20–25 minutes or until the chicken is cooked through. Brush with the glaze two or three times while cooking.

GROWN-UPS
Calories 250; Calories from fat 70
Total fat 7 g; Saturated fat 1.5 g
Cholesterol 80 mg; Sodium 560 mg
Carbohydrate 20 g; Dietary fiber 0 g
Sugars 17 g; Protein 26 g

CHILDREN
Calories 110; Calories from fat 20
Total fat 2.5 g; Saturated fat 0.5 g
Cholesterol 40 mg; Sodium 40 mg
Carbohydrate 9 g; Dietary fiber 0 g
Sugars 8 g; Protein 13 g

Teriyaki Honey Glazed Drumettes: Substitute chicken wings or drumettes for the drumsticks. Makes a great appetizer.

Teriyaki Honey Glazed Hens: Split Cornish game hens in half. Remove the skin. Glaze and bake for 35–45 minutes. Makes a great entrée for entertaining.

INDONESIAN CHICKEN SATAY
& TERIYAKI CHICKEN SATAY

Time to table: 25–30 minutes   Serves 2 adults and 2 or 3 children

An Indonesian specialty, satay is usually served as an appetizer but here it is used as the main course. Marinated chicken is skewered then grilled. The accompanying spicy peanut sauce is traditional. Since my children love peanut butter, their mildly flavored sauce was a big hit. Grill the satay outside in the summer or broil indoors in the winter. This entrée goes well with Lime Cilantro Pilaf, Sesame Oriental Rice, Orange Ginger Glazed Carrots or Asparagus, and Orange Sesame Snowpeas.

❝Very different from what I usually make for dinner. We liked it very much. My youngest loved the skewers.❞

3–4 skinned and boned chicken
   breast halves, about 1¼ pounds

GROWN-UPS
¼ cup light teriyaki marinade
1 tablespoon fresh lemon juice
½ teaspoon grated fresh ginger

¼–½ teaspoon red chili sauce or
   crushed red pepper
Salt and pepper to taste

CHILDREN
¼ cup light teriyaki marinade
Salt to taste

Start the coals of an outdoor grill or set oven to broil.

Wash the chicken and pat dry. Cut into ¼-inch strips. Divide in half and place into different bowls.

Pour the teriyaki marinade over the children's portions and mix well.

Combine the teriyaki marinade, lemon juice, ginger, and chili sauce. Pour over the grown-ups' portions and mix well. Marinate for 10 minutes or more.

Thread the chicken on metal skewers. Season the skewers for the grown-ups with salt and pepper. Season the skewers for the children with salt. Grill or broil for 2–3 minutes on each side or until the chicken is cooked through. Serve with the Peanut Sauce.

PEANUT SAUCE

¼ cup smooth peanut butter
⅓ cup rice vinegar
2 garlic cloves, minced
2 tablespoons light soy sauce
1 tablespoon honey

GROWN-UPS
½ teaspoon grated fresh ginger
¼–½ teaspoon red chili sauce or
  crushed red pepper

Mix together the peanut butter, rice vinegar, garlic, soy sauce, and honey. Pour half of the peanut sauce into another bowl for the children. Mix the remaining sauce with the ginger and chili for the grown-ups.

GROWN-UPS
Calories 320; Calories from fat 90
Total fat 10 g; Saturated fat 2.5 g
Cholesterol 100 mg; Sodium 550 mg
Carbohydrate 11 g; Dietary fiber 1 g
Sugars 6 g; Protein 44 g

CHILDREN
Calories 220; Calories from fat 60
Total fat 7 g; Saturated fat 1.5 g
Cholesterol 65 mg; Sodium 570 mg
Carbohydrate 9 g; Dietary fiber 0 g
Sugars 7 g; Protein 30 g

Indonesian Beef Satay: Substitute beef for the chicken.
Indonesian Shrimp Satay: Substitute shrimp for the chicken.

CAJUN SPICED CHICKEN & CRUNCHY

CHICKEN NUGGETS

Time to table: 30–35 minutes   Serves 2 adults and 2 or 3 children

This chicken is oven-fried but still has the crunchy texture of deep-fat-fried chicken. The crisp crust is made from corn-flakes. To assure that the chicken cooks quickly, remove the tender-loin from the rib side of the chicken breast. If the chicken is unusually thick, pound it with the flat side of a meat mallet to thin it out. The children's variation is cut into nuggets or cookie-cutter shapes, time permitting. It's easy—just pound the chicken to an even thickness. Place a metal cookie cutter on the chicken and tap with a tenderizing mallet. Trim if necessary with a sharp paring knife and reshape on the baking dish after coating. This recipe goes well with Garlic Mashed Potatoes, Cilantro Pesto Corn on the Cob, and Honey Mustard Green Bean Salad.

> ❝We'll add this to our collection of recipes since we
> eat a ton of chicken.❞

Vegetable cooking spray
4 boneless and skinless chicken
  breast halves, about 1½ pounds
4 cups cornflakes

GROWN-UPS
Salt and pepper to taste
2 teaspoons Cajun spice mix
  (see note)

2 tablespoons ketchup
1 teaspoon extra-hot Chinese-style
  mustard

CHILDREN
Salt to taste
1–2 tablespoons ketchup

Preheat oven to 425 degrees F. Coat a large baking sheet with cooking spray and set aside.

Rinse the chicken under cold water and pat dry. Season the chicken for the grown-ups with salt and pepper. Cut half of the chicken into nuggets or other shapes, if desired. Season with salt.

Place the cornflakes in a heavy-duty plastic bag. Squeeze out any excess air and seal. Finely crush the cornflakes with a rolling pin. Transfer the mixture to a pie pan and set aside.

Put the nuggets in a bowl and add the ketchup. Mix until the nuggets are coated. Roll them in the cornflakes, four to five at a time, until well coated. Gently place on the prepared baking sheet. Repeat until all the nuggets are coated. Lightly spray with cooking spray.

Add the Cajun spice mix to the remaining cornflake mixture and stir to combine. Mix the ketchup and mustard together in a small bowl. Spoon some of the ketchup on one side of a chicken breast. Place the chicken, ketchup side down, into the seasoned cornflakes. Spoon more ketchup on the other side. Roll in the cornflakes until well coated. Gently place on the baking sheet with the nuggets. Repeat the same process with the remaining chicken breast. Lightly coat the chicken with cooking spray.

Place the baking sheet in the oven and bake until cooked through, 15–20 minutes for the Chicken Nuggets and 20–25 minutes for the Cajun Spiced Chicken.

GROWN-UPS	CHILDREN
Calories 250; Calories from fat 20	Calories 170; Calories from fat 15
Total fat 2.5 g; Saturated fat 0.5 g	Total fat 1.5 g; Saturated fat 0 g
Cholesterol 100 mg; Sodium 520 mg	Cholesterol 65 mg; Sodium 350 mg
Carbohydrate 16 g; Dietary fiber 0 g	Carbohydrate 10 g; Dietary fiber 0 g
Sugars 3 g; Protein 41 g	Sugars 2 g; Protein 27 g

Note: Commercial Cajun spice mixes can be purchased ready-made. To make your own, combine: 3 tablespoons sweet paprika, 2 teaspoons onion powder, 2 teaspoons garlic powder, 2 teaspoons ground black pepper, 2 teaspoons ground white pepper, 2 teaspoons cayenne, 1 teaspoon ground thyme, 1 teaspoon ground oregano, and 1 teaspoon celery salt. Store in a tightly covered container. Makes about ⅓ cup.

SHANGHAI CHICKEN KABOBS

& MINI CHICKEN KABOBS

Time to table: 25–30 minutes   Serves 2 adults and 2 to 4 children

My children are always delighted when served their favorite foods on skewers. With kabobs, everyone gets a personal serving. The food is already cut up into bite-size pieces, easy for kids to eat. Sometimes I carry the theme through to other parts of the meal: skewered cherry tomatoes and cucumber wedges make a delightful salad, or skewered fresh peach slices and strawberries make a great dessert.

For the mini kabobs, use the small 6-inch skewers with chicken only or alternate with pineapple and pepper if to the children's liking. For the grown-ups, use 10-inch skewers. Fresh pineapple adds a nice touch to this dish but use canned when fresh is not available or time is limited. This recipes goes well with Sesame Oriental Rice, Teriyaki Sesame Broccoli or Asparagus, and Lime Cilantro Pilaf.

½ pound boneless and skinless
  chicken breast and ½ pound
  thigh meat
Salt to taste
1–2 cups fresh or canned pineapple
  chunks
1 or 2 red or green bell peppers,
  cut into 1-inch pieces
¼ cup light teriyaki marinade
2 tablespoons orange or pineapple
  juice concentrate, thawed

GROWN-UPS
1 teaspoon Chinese five-spice
  powder (see note)
1 teaspoon turmeric
½ teaspoon coriander
¼ teaspoon onion powder
¼ teaspoon garlic powder
⅛ teaspoon cayenne

Set oven to broil. Line a broiler pan with aluminum foil and set aside.

Wash the chicken and pat dry. Cut the chicken into bite-size chunks. Season with salt.

For the children, thread the chicken on 6-inch skewers, alternating with pineapple chunks and bell pepper, if desired. Mix the teriyaki sauce and orange juice concentrate together. Brush over the kabobs and place on the broiler pan.

Combine the Chinese five-spice powder with turmeric, coriander, onion powder, garlic powder, and cayenne. Season the chicken for the grown-ups with the mixture. Thread the chicken on 10-inch skewers alternating with pineapple chunks and bell peppers. Brush with the teriyaki-orange sauce. Place the kabobs on the broiler pan and broil for 5–6 minutes on each side, or until the chicken is cooked through.

Note: Chinese five-spice powder is a blend of spices used throughout China and Vietnam. It can be found in the spice section of most supermarkets

GROWN-UPS
Calories 200; Calories from fat 15
Total fat 2 g; Saturated fat 0 g
Cholesterol 65 mg; Sodium 560 mg
Carbohydrate 18 g; Dietary fiber 2 g
Sugars 14 g; Protein 28 g

CHILDREN
Calories 110; Calories from fat 20
Total fat 2.5 g; Saturated fat 0.5 g
Cholesterol 45 mg; Sodium 390 mg
Carbohydrate 9 g; Dietary fiber 0 g
Sugars 7 g; Protein 12 g

CHICKEN IN CHIPOTLE CHILE
··
BARBECUE SAUCE & CHICKEN WITH
··
SWEET BARBECUE SAUCE
··

Time to table: 25–30 minutes   Serves 2 adults and 2 to 4 children

For the children, chicken is slathered with a more traditional barbecue sauce made with pineapple and maple syrup. For the grownups, the secret to this spicy, sweet, and smoky-flavored sauce is chipotle chiles (smoked jalapeño peppers). They can be found in the ethnic food section of some supermarkets and Latino or gourmet food stores, and are available in a variety of forms including dried, canned, and puréed. They are so spicy that only one or two are needed to flavor an entire dish. If using canned, divide the remaining chiles in small packages and freeze for use in other recipes. If using dried, simmer in boiling water for 10–15 minutes to soften. If chipotle chiles are impossible to find in your area, substitute ¼–½ teaspoon liquid smoke and ½–1 tablespoon chopped, canned, or jarred jalapeño peppers. This entrée goes well with Rosemary or Thyme Roasted New Potatoes, Cilantro Pesto Corn on the Cob, or Cajun Fried Zucchini.

❝This was a terrific alternative to our chicken recipes. My kids generally don't like chicken but loved this.❞

2 boneless, skinless chicken breast
    halves, about ¾ pound
2–4 boneless, skinless chicken
    thighs
1 medium yellow onion, minced,
    about 1 cup
1 large rib celery, chopped very
    fine, about ⅓ cup
¼ cup maple syrup
2 teaspoons dry mustard
3 tablespoons Worcestershire sauce

1 8-ounce can crushed pineapple
    with juice
1 6-ounce can tomato paste
3 tablespoons lemon juice

GROWN-UPS
Salt and pepper to taste
1 or 2 chipotle chiles in adobo
    sauce, finely chopped

CHILDREN
Salt to taste

Rinse the chicken and pat dry. Remove the tenderloin from the rib side of the chicken. Season the chicken breast and tenderloins for the grown-ups with salt and pepper. Season the chicken thighs for the children with salt, if desired. Heat a large nonstick skillet for 2 minutes over medium-high heat. Place the chicken into the skillet so that the pieces do not overlap. Cook for 4–5 minutes on each side or until done.

Remove the chicken from the skillet. Transfer to an ovenproof dish and keep warm in the oven. Add the onions and celery to the skillet and stir for 2–3 minutes. Add the maple syrup, mustard, Worcestershire sauce, pineapple, tomato paste, and lemon juice. Stir to combine. Bring the mixture to a boil, reduce heat, cover, and simmer for 5 minutes. Transfer a portion of the sauce to small bowls for the children.

Stir 1 chipotle chile into the sauce. Taste for spiciness and add more, if desired. Remove the chicken breast meat from the oven and transfer to the skillet. Spoon the sauce over the chicken and simmer for 5 minutes. Serve the chicken thighs with the sauce on the side for dipping.

GROWN-UPS	CHILDREN
Calories 320; Calories from fat 25	Calories 150; Calories from fat 30
Total fat 3 g; Saturated fat 0.5 g	Total fat 3 g; Saturated fat 0.5 g
Cholesterol 100 mg; Sodium 270 mg	Cholesterol 55 mg; Sodium 140 mg
Carbohydrate 32 g; Dietary fiber 3 g	Carbohydrate 16 g; Dietary fiber 1 g
Sugars 20 g; Protein 42 g	Sugars 10 g; Protein 15 g

HOISIN GLAZED CHICKEN & HONEY
ORANGE GLAZED CHICKEN

Time to table: 30–35 minutes   **Serves 2 adults and 2 to 4 children**

Here chicken is prepared with a simple glaze and broiled. For the grown-ups, store-bought hoisin sauce is combined with rice vinegar and red chili sauce to produce a spicy, sweet-and-sour glaze. For the children, honey, orange juice, and a touch of soy sauce make a deliciously sweet glaze. This dish goes well with Sesame Oriental Rice, Teriyaki Sesame Broccoli or Asparagus, and Orange Sesame Snowpeas.

Simple and delicious. We eat a lot of Asian food. The kids liked the adult version better but not quite so hot.

2 boneless, skinless chicken breast halves, about ¾ pound

4 chicken thighs, without or with skin

¼ teaspoon each: salt, pepper, garlic powder, and onion powder

GROWN-UPS

1 tablespoon rice vinegar

1 tablespoon hoisin sauce

½–1 teaspoon red chili sauce

CHILDREN

1 tablespoon honey

1 tablespoon orange juice concentrate, thawed

1 teaspoon soy sauce

Set oven to broil. Line broiler pan with aluminum foil.

Rinse the chicken under cold water and pat dry. Remove the tenderloin from the rib side of the chicken breast. Season the chicken pieces with salt, pepper, garlic powder, and onion powder, omitting any that they dislike from the children's portions.

Mix together the rice vinegar, hoisin sauce, and red chili sauce in a small bowl. Brush the sauce on both sides of the chicken breast and tenderloin. Place on the broiler pan.

Mix together the honey, orange juice concentrate, and soy sauce in a small bowl. Spread the sauce on both sides of the chicken thighs. Place on the broiler pan.

Broil the chicken for 5–6 minutes, turn it over, and brush again with the glaze. Broil for another 4–5 minutes, until cooked through.

GROWN-UPS
Calories 210; Calories from fat 20
Total fat 2.5 g; Saturated fat 0.5 g
Cholesterol 100 mg; Sodium 380 mg
Carbohydrate 5 g; Dietary fiber 0 g
Sugars 4 g; Protein 40 g

CHILDREN
Calories 110; Calories from fat 25
Total fat 2.5 g; Saturated fat 0.5 g
Cholesterol 55 mg; Sodium 60 mg
Carbohydrate 6 g; Dietary fiber 0 g
Sugars 6 g; Protein 14 g

Hoisin Glazed Pork Chops: Substitute center-cut pork chops for the chicken. Trim away excess fat. Brush the hoisin glaze on the pork chops and broil for 5–6 minutes on each side.

LEMON ROSEMARY ROAST CHICKEN
& LEMON HERB ROAST CHICKEN

Time to table: 30–35 minutes   **Serves 2 adults and 2 to 4 children**

For the grown-ups, fresh rosemary, lemon, and garlic make a perfect combination for seasoning chicken. The seasonings are tucked under the skin while roasting to keep the meat moist. The skin is then removed before serving. For the children, fines herbes, a delicate blend of herbs, is used instead of rosemary. This recipe goes well with Garlic Mashed Potatoes, Greek-Style Green Beans, Parsley Creamed Corn, and Honey Mustard Acorn Squash.

*2 boneless chicken breast halves
    with skin*
*2–4 chicken drumsticks or thighs
    with skin, if desired*
4 medium garlic cloves, minced
2 teaspoons grated lemon zest

½ teaspoon salt
1 teaspoon fines herbes (see note)

GROWN-UPS
*1 tablespoon fresh chopped
    rosemary or ½ tablespoon dried*

Preheat oven to 450 degrees F. Coat a baking dish with cooking spray.

Rinse the chicken in cold water and pat dry.

Combine the garlic, lemon zest, salt, and fines herbes. Rub about half of the herb mixture on the drumsticks, and place them in the roasting pan.

Add the rosemary to the remaining mixture. Loosen the skin from the chicken breasts. Place the mixture under the skin. Insert toothpicks to hold the skin in place while roasting. Transfer to the roasting pan.

Roast for 20–25 minutes. Remove the skin from the chicken breasts before serving.

Note: Fines herbes is a traditional French blend of subtle herbs including parsley, chervil, chives, and tarragon. It can be found already blended in the spice section at most supermarkets.

GROWN-UPS
Calories 260; Calories from fat 60
Total fat 6 g; Saturated fat 3.5 g
Cholesterol 100 mg; Sodium 400 mg
Carbohydrate 7 g; Dietary fiber 0 g
Sugars 7 g; Protein 42 g

CHILDREN
Calories 90; Calories from fat 25
Total fat 2.5 g; Saturated fat 0.5 g
Cholesterol 55 mg; Sodium 210 mg
Carbohydrate 1 g; Dietary fiber 0 g
Sugars 0 g; Protein 14 g

Lemon Thyme Roast Chicken: Substitute chopped fresh thyme for the rosemary.

GRILLED GREEK CHICKEN
WITH FETA SAUCE &
GRILLED PARMESAN CHICKEN

Time to table: 20–25 minutes   Serves 2 adults and 2 to 4 children

C hicken is sprinkled with a Mediterranean-style seasoning, then pan-fried. For the children, the chicken is lightly seasoned with herbs and Parmesan cheese. For the grown-ups, the pan juices are deglazed with balsamic vinegar and thickened with feta cheese to create a sweet and pungent sauce. This recipe goes well with Rosemary Roasted New Potatoes, Dilly Green Beans, and Greek-Style Green Beans.

❝*Simple and easy to make. Loved the flavors.*❞

2 boneless and skinless chicken
   breast halves
4 boneless and skinless chicken
   thighs
¼ teaspoon of each: salt, pepper,
   garlic powder, and onion powder

GROWN-UPS
½ teaspoon crumbled dried oregano

¼ cup balsamic vinegar
2 tablespoons apple juice
1 tablespoon capers, rinsed and
   drained
¼ cup crumbled feta cheese

CHILDREN
½ teaspoon fines herbes
2 tablespoons Parmesan cheese

Heat a large nonstick skillet over medium-high heat for 2 minutes. Remove the tenderloin from the rib side of the breasts. Season the breast and tenderloin with salt, pepper, garlic powder, onion powder, and oregano. Season the chicken thighs for the children with salt, garlic powder, onion powder, and fines herbes, omitting any that the children dislike.

Pan-fry the chicken pieces for 4–5 minutes per side. Remove the chicken from the pan. Pour in the balsamic vinegar and apple juice, scraping the bottom of the pan to loosen browned bits of chicken and seasonings. Add the capers and cheese and stir until heated through, about 45 seconds. Pour the sauce over the chicken for the grown-ups and serve immediately. Serve the chicken thighs topped with Parmesan cheese.

GROWN-UPS
Calories 260; Calories from fat 60
Total fat 6 g; Saturated fat 3.5 g
Cholesterol 115 mg; Sodium 490 mg
Carbohydrate 7 g; Dietary fiber 0 g
Sugars 7 g; Protein 42 g

CHILDREN
Calories 100; Calories from fat 35
Total fat 3.5 g; Saturated fat 1.5 g
Cholesterol 60 mg; Sodium 115 mg
Carbohydrate 0 g; Dietary fiber 0 g
Sugars 0 g; Protein 15 g

CHICKEN WITH CAPERS AND
SUN-DRIED TOMATOES
& CHICKEN PARMIGIANA

Time to table: 20–25 minutes   Serves 2 adults and 2 to 4 children

E asy and quick, this chicken dish is full of flavor. For the children, pizza sauce and mozzarella cheese cover the chicken. For the grown-ups, the distinctive Mediterranean flavors come from capers, sun-dried tomatoes, oregano, and balsamic vinegar. This entrée goes well with Lemon Parsley Couscous, Rosemary Roasted New Potatoes, and Thyme Roasted Carrots.

2 boneless and skinless chicken
  breast halves, about ¾ pound
4 boneless and skinless chicken
  thighs
¼ teaspoon of each: salt, pepper,
  garlic powder, and onion powder

GROWN-UPS
1 teaspoon olive oil
2 garlic cloves, minced
1 teaspoon dried oregano

¼ cup oil-packed sun-dried
  tomatoes, well rinsed and
  drained
1 green onion, sliced
1 tablespoon capers, well rinsed
  and chopped
2 tablespoons balsamic vinegar

CHILDREN
1 cup pizza or spaghetti sauce
¼ cup grated mozzarella cheese

Heat a large nonstick skillet over medium-high heat for 2 minutes. Remove the tenderloin from the rib side of the chicken breasts. Rinse the chicken and pat dry. Season the breasts and tenderloins for the grown-ups with salt, pepper, garlic powder, and onion powder. Season the chicken thighs for the children with salt, garlic powder, and onion powder, if acceptable. Pan-fry the chicken for 4–5 minutes per side, until cooked through.

Transfer the chicken thighs to a microwave-safe dish. Pour the pizza sauce over the chicken, cover, and microwave at full power for 2–3 minutes. Sprinkle the cheese over the top.

Transfer the chicken for the grown-ups to individual plates or a serving platter. Pour the olive oil into the center of the skillet. Add the garlic and oregano, stirring for 30–45 seconds, until fragrant. Add the sun-dried tomatoes, green onions, and capers. Add the balsamic vinegar to the skillet, scraping the bottom of the pan to loosen browned bits of chicken and seasonings. Heat through and spoon the sauce over the adult servings.

GROWN-UPS
Calories 240; Calories from fat 40
Total fat 4.5 g; Saturated fat 1 g
Cholesterol 100 mg; Sodium 100 mg
Carbohydrate 8 g; Dietary fiber 1 g
Sugars 5 g; Protein 41 g

CHILDREN
Calories 110; Calories from fat 30
Total fat 3.5 g; Saturated fat 0.5 g
Cholesterol 55 mg; Sodium 350 mg
Carbohydrate 4 g; Dietary fiber 1 g
Sugars 3 g; Protein 15 g

CHINESE CHICKEN VEGETABLE WRAPS & SALSA CHICKEN VEGETABLE WRAPS

Time to table: 25–30 minutes   Serves 2 adults and 2 to 4 children

This is a twist on traditional chicken burritos. For the grown-ups, Asian-style seasonings are used for flavor. For the children, a more traditional Mexican-style burrito is made using cheese and salsa. This dish goes well with Mixed Citrus Salad, Orange Ginger Red Cabbage Slaw, and Citrus Jicama Slaw.

1 cup white rice
4 burrito-size nonfat or low-fat
    flour tortillas
2 boneless and skinless chicken
    breast halves, about ¾ pound
¼ teaspoon of each: salt, onion
    powder, and garlic powder
2 cups fresh asparagus or broccoli,
    cut into small pieces

GROWN-UPS
2 tablespoons ketchup
2 tablespoons hoisin sauce
2 tablespoons toasted sesame seeds

CHILDREN
⅓ cup shredded Monterey Jack
    or Cheddar cheese
¼ cup mild salsa

**"My husband and I really like the Asian seasonings.
Our kids were perfectly happy with the Mexican-style
burritos, with which they are more familiar."**

Prepare the rice according to package directions.

Preheat oven to 350 degrees F.

Using a pastry brush, brush the tortillas with water, or rinse them under running water and shake off excess. Stack the tortillas and seal in aluminum foil. Place in the oven to heat for 10–15 minutes.

Rinse the chicken under cold water and pat dry. Cut into thin strips. Season with salt, onion powder, and garlic powder. Heat a large non-stick skillet over medium-high heat for 2 minutes. Place the chicken strips into the skillet so that the pieces do not overlap. Stir for 4–5 minutes until cooked through.

Place the vegetables in a microwave-safe dish. Add a few table-spoons of water, cover with plastic wrap, and microwave at full power for 3 minutes. Let stand, covered, for 3 minutes.

While the vegetables are cooking, mix together the ketchup and hoisin sauce.

To serve, place the tortillas, rice, chicken, asparagus, ketchup/hoisin sauce, sesame seeds, cheese, and salsa on the table. Allow each person to make individual wraps with favored fillings. Suggested fillings: For the Chinese Chicken Vegetable Wraps include rice, chicken, asparagus, ketchup/hoisin sauce, and sesame seeds. For the Salsa Chicken Wraps, include rice, chicken, asparagus, cheese, and salsa.

GROWN-UPS

Calories 480; Calories from fat 30
Total fat 3 g; Saturated fat 1 g
Cholesterol 50 mg; Sodium 840 mg
Carbohydrate 78 g; Dietary fiber 3 g
Sugars 4 g; Protein 29 g

CHILDREN

Calories 250; Calories from fat 35
Total fat 4 g; Saturated fat 2 g
Cholesterol 35 mg; Sodium 350 mg
Carbohydrate 35 g; Dietary fiber 1 g
Sugars 2 g; Protein 17 g

ASIAN MEAT LOAF

& MINI MEAT LOAVES

Time to table: 25 minutes   Serves 3 adults and 3 to 6 children

Meat loaf is as American as apple pie, but in this recipe, ginger, soy sauce, and water chestnuts add a distinctive Asian accent to the grown-ups' variation. For the children, the preparation is more traditional. Ground turkey breast is used to keep the fat content low. Oatmeal is used to keep the meat loaf moist. Once mixed, the meat loaf is packed into 6-ounce custard cups and cooked in the microwave. This goes well with Orange Ginger Glazed Carrots, Orange Sesame Snowpeas, and Teriyaki Sesame Broccoli.

❝*This was delicious and really fast for meat loaf. I chopped all the vegetables in the food processor. It took no time at all. Everyone liked the individual servings.*❞

1 egg
¼ cup low-fat milk
⅓ cup rolled oats
1 pound ground turkey breast
⅓ cup ketchup
½ teaspoon celery salt
3 green onions, sliced
2 carrots, peeled and chopped
1 celery rib, chopped
2 garlic cloves, minced
1 8-ounce can sliced water
  chestnuts, drained and chopped

GROWN-UPS
½ teaspoon ground ginger
2 tablespoons light soy sauce
2 tablespoons ketchup
1 teaspoon extra-hot Chinese-style
  mustard

CHILDREN
2 tablespoons ketchup

Scramble the egg and milk together in a medium-size mixing bowl. Add the oats, turkey, ketchup, and celery salt, stirring to combine.

Prepare the green onions, carrots, celery, water chestnuts, and garlic by hand or in the food processor. You may do this all in one batch if the children like them all or in separate batches, adding only what the children like to their variation.

If the children like all of the vegetables, mix the vegetables together with the turkey in one bowl. Otherwise, separate the mixture, adding only the vegetables that the children like.

To half of the meat mixture, add the ginger and soy sauce, stirring to combine. Pack into three 6-ounce custard cups.

Pack the meat loaf for the children into three custard cups.

Place the custard cups in the microwave oven. Place a piece of wax paper or plastic wrap loosely over the top. Microwave at full power for 10–12 minutes, rotating the custard cups halfway through.

Remove from the oven. Glaze the tops of the meat loaves for the children with ketchup. Mix the ketchup and Chinese mustard together. Glaze the tops of the meat loaves for the grownups with the mixture.

GROWN-UPS
Calories 220; Calories from fat 20
Total fat 2.5 g; Saturated fat 0.5 g
Cholesterol 95 mg; Sodium 760 mg
Carbohydrate 23 g; Dietary fiber 3 g
Sugars 6 g; Protein 22 g

CHILDREN
Calories 100; Calories from fat 10
Total fat 1 g; Saturated fat 0 g
Cholesterol 45 mg; Sodium 270 mg
Carbohydrate 11 g; Dietary fiber 20 g
Sugars 3 g; Protein 11 g

ITALIAN TURKEY MEAT LOAF &
....
CHEESY ITALIAN TURKEY MEAT LOAF
....

Time to table: 25 minutes   Serves 3 adults and 3 to 6 children

This more traditionally seasoned meat loaf is a family favorite. Made with ground turkey or extra-lean ground beef, meat loaf is a great way to sneak a few vegetables into the children's meal. Use the food processor to chop the vegetables very fine so that they blend well with the other ingredients. This entrée goes well with Garlic Mashed Potatoes, Rosemary Roasted New Potatoes, and Dilly Green Beans.

1 egg
½ cup milk
½ teaspoon salt
1 teaspoon Italian seasoning
2 slices white bread
1 pound ground turkey breast
1 15-ounce can pizza sauce

1 medium onion, chopped
1 carrot, peeled and chopped
1 celery stalk, chopped
2 garlic cloves, minced

CHILDREN
3 slices American cheese

In a large mixing bowl, whisk together the egg, milk, salt, and Italian seasoning until well blended.

Remove the crust from the bread slices and cut into 1/2-inch cubes. Add to egg mixture and toss until well coated. Add the ground turkey and 2/3 of the can of pizza sauce. Stir until well combined. Transfer half of the mixture to another bowl.

Add the onions, carrots, celery, and garlic to both meat loaf mixtures, omitting any that the children find objectionable. (If the children like all of the vegetables, it is not necessary to divide the mixture in half.)

Pack the meat loaf for the grown-ups into three 6-ounce custard cups. Pack the meat loaf for the children into three custard cups. Place in the microwave oven and cover loosely with wax paper or plastic wrap. Microwave at full power for 10–12 minutes, rotating the dishes halfway through. Run a knife around the edges of the cups and invert onto a microwave-safe plate. Top the children's meat loaves with a slice of American cheese. Microwave for 20–25 seconds so that the cheese melts. Top the meat loaves with the remaining pizza sauce.

GROWN-UPS
Calories 200; Calories from fat 35
Total fat 3.5 g; Saturated fat 1 g
Cholesterol 95 mg; Sodium 710 mg
Carbohydrate 17 g; Dietary fiber 2 g
Sugars 9 g; Protein 24 g

CHILDREN
Calories 100; Calories from fat 15
Total fat 2 g; Saturated fat 0.5 g
Cholesterol 50 mg; Sodium 360 mg
Carbohydrate 8 g; Dietary fiber 1 g
Sugars 4 g; Protein 12 g

STUFFED BELL PEPPERS WITH
GREEN CHILE SPANISH RICE &
SWEET TOMATO RICE

Time to table: 30 minutes   Serves 2 adults and 2 children

Bell peppers have a mild tang and crunchy texture. Their size, shape, and firmness make them a perfect container to hold fillings. While some children may prefer red over green, others may object to peppers entirely. For them the solution is simple—skip the peppers altogether. The pizza-flavored rice can be packed into custard cups. Serve in the cup or unmold on the plate. This recipe goes well with Mixed Citrus Salad, Citrus Jicama Slaw, or Honey Mustard Mixed Bean Salad.

“We liked the stuffed peppers—used red because they are sweeter. For the kids, I used custard cups and they really like it.”

2 to 4 medium-size bell peppers
½ pound ground turkey breast or
   ground sirloin
3 garlic cloves, minced
1 15-ounce can pizza sauce or
   spaghetti sauce
½ cup water
1 cup instant rice

½ cup grated Monterey Jack cheese
Grated Monterey Jack cheese for
   garnish

GROWN-UPS
1 teaspoon chili powder
1 3- or 4-ounce can chopped green
   chiles, mild, medium, or hot

Cut off the stem end of each pepper. Remove the seeds and membranes. Rinse the peppers and place in a microwave-safe baking dish. Cover with vented plastic wrap and microwave at full power for 3½ minutes. Set aside.

Heat a nonstick skillet over medium-high heat for 2 minutes. Add the turkey and garlic. With a wooden spoon, break the turkey into small pieces and stir until cooked through. Pour the pizza sauce and water into the skillet; bring to a boil. Stir in the rice, cover, remove from heat, and let stand for 5 minutes.

Stir in the cheese and stuff the children's peppers, if using, or pack into two 8-ounce custard cups. Reheat in the microwave for 2–3 minutes. Serve in the custard cups or unmold onto dinner plates.

Stir the chili powder and green chiles into the remaining rice mixture. Pack into the bell peppers and put back into the baking dish. Place any remaining rice on the bottom of the dish. Cover with plastic wrap and microwave at full power for 3–4 minutes to heat through.

GROWN-UPS
Calories 300; Calories from fat 60
Total fat 7 g; Saturated fat 3 g
Cholesterol 50 mg; Sodium 700 mg
Carbohydrate 36 g; Dietary fiber 5 g
Sugars 8 g; Protein 22 g

CHILDREN
Calories 300; Calories from fat 60
Total fat 7 g; Saturated fat 3 g
Cholesterol 50 mg; Sodium 700 mg
Carbohydrate 36 g; Dietary fiber 5 g
Sugars 8 g; Protein 22 g

VEGETABLE MAIN DISHES

STUFFED ZUCCHINI WITH
MEDITERRANEAN COUSCOUS
& PARMESAN COUSCOUS

Time to table: 25 minutes   Serves 2 adults and 2 children

In this recipe, zucchini are hollowed out to form a container that holds the Mediterranean-style filling. This simple vegetarian main course packs a lot of flavor from Greek olives, capers, and fresh dill. Rinse the olives and capers under cold water; otherwise the dish can be too salty. Mild-tasting zucchini does not dominate the flavor, although some children may object to finding their main course stuffed inside one. As an alternative, pack the stuffing into custard cups. Instant rice can be substituted for the couscous, if desired. This dish goes well with Honey Mustard Mixed Bean Salad or Garlic Roasted Broccoli.

2 to 4 medium-size zucchini
   squash, about ⅓ pound each
Salt and pepper to taste
¼ cup minced onions
2 garlic cloves, minced
1 15-ounce can spaghetti sauce or
   pizza sauce
½ cup water

1 cup couscous
¼ cup Parmesan cheese

GROWN-UPS
8 pitted Greek olives, well rinsed
   and chopped
1 tablespoon capers, well rinsed
   and chopped
1½ tablespoons chopped fresh dill

My husband really enjoyed this. We try to eat a vegetarian meal at least once a week. The kids are not big vegetable fans, but they liked the boat-shaped zucchini.

Rinse the zucchini and trim both ends. With a spoon, carefully scoop out the insides, leaving 1/4-inch on all sides to form a shell. Season with salt and pepper and place the zucchini on a microwave-safe plate. Cover with plastic wrap and microwave at full power for 5–6 minutes, rotating the dish after 3 minutes. Do this in batches if the microwave is not large enough to hold all the pieces.

Finely chop the insides of the zucchini. Heat a nonstick saucepan over medium heat for 2 minutes. Add the chopped zucchini, onion, and garlic. Stir until soft, about 5 minutes. Add the spaghetti sauce and water. Bring to a boil, stir in the couscous, remove from the heat, cover, and let stand for 5 minutes. Fluff with a fork and fold in the Parmesan cheese. Use this mixture to fill the zucchini for the children or pack into 8-ounce custard cups. Reheat in the microwave at full power for 2–3 minutes. Serve in custard cups or unmold onto dinner plates.

To the remaining couscous mixture, stir in the olives, capers, and dill. Stuff the zucchini for the grown-ups with this mixture. Reheat the stuffed zucchini in the microwave for 2–3 minutes.

GROWN-UPS
Calories 290; Calories from fat 50
Total fat 6 g; Saturated fat 2 g
Cholesterol 5 mg; Sodium 740 mg
Carbohydrate 47 g; Dietary fiber 6 g
Sugars 8 g; Protein 11 g

CHILDREN
Calories 270; Calories from fat 35
Total fat 4 g; Saturated fat 1.5 g
Cholesterol 5 mg; Sodium 530 mg
Carbohydrate 46 g; Dietary fiber 5 g
Sugars 7 g; Protein 11 g

ROASTED RED PEPPER QUESADILLAS
···
& CHEESE QUESADILLAS
···

Time to table: 20–25 minutes   Serves 2 adults and 2 to 4 children

Quesadillas, like tacos or burritos, can be customized to meet a variety of taste preferences. For the kids, stuff flour tortillas with cheese, or make the quesadillas more elaborate by including other ingredients that they like. For the grown-ups, to keep the calories and fat low, go easy on the cheese. Use just a small amount to "glue" the filling ingredients together. These go well with Green Chile Rice, Mixed Citrus Salad, and Lime Cilantro Pilaf.

❝Very easy to make variations for kids
and adults—tasty too.❞

4 large nonfat or low-fat flour
   tortillas
4 ounces grated low-fat Monterey
   Jack or Mexican-style cheese,
   about 1 cup
1 15-ounce can black beans,
   rinsed and drained
4 green onions, chopped fine

¼ bunch cilantro, chopped
¼–½ cup salsa, roasted garlic or
   other gourmet flavor

GROWN-UPS
1 7¼-ounce jar roasted red
   peppers, rinsed, drained, and
   chopped

Heat a large nonstick skillet over medium-high heat for 1 minute. Place a tortilla in the skillet. To make the children's variation, place cheese and any other ingredients that they like on the tortilla. Heat until the cheese melts and the tortilla is lightly browned. Fold the tortilla in half like an omelette. Place the quesadillas in a warm oven until ready to serve. To make the adult variation, use cheese, peppers, black beans, onions, cilantro, and salsa for the filling. Cut the quesadillas into wedges for serving.

GROWN-UPS	CHILDREN
Calories 380; Calories from fat 60	Calories 230; Calories from fat 50
Total fat 7 g; Saturated fat 4.5 g	Total fat 6 g; Saturated fat 4 g
Cholesterol 20 mg; Sodium 870 mg	Cholesterol 20 mg; Sodium 560 mg
Carbohydrate 54 g; Dietary fiber 9 g	Carbohydrate 27 g; Dietary fiber 0 g
Sugars 6 g; Protein 22 g	Sugars 1 g; Protein 13 g

SPAGHETTI SQUASH WITH SPINACH WALNUT SAGE PESTO & SPAGHETTI SQUASH WITH MARINARA SAUCE

Time to table: 25–30 minutes   **Serves 2 adults and 2 or 3 children**

Spaghetti squash is unique among squashes: When cooked, the pulp can be pulled apart to form slender strands that resemble spaghetti. And even better, an 8-ounce serving has only 75 calories. For the grown-ups, an earthy flavored pesto made from spinach, walnuts, and fresh sage accentuates the squash flavor. For the children, the spaghetti squash is topped with plenty of marinara sauce and Parmesan cheese. This dish goes well with Dilly Green Beans, Mixed Citrus Salad, or Honey Mustard Mixed Bean Salad.

1 small spaghetti squash, about 2–3 pounds
Freshly grated Parmesan cheese for garnish
Salt and pepper to taste

GROWN-UPS
Walnut Sage Pesto (recipe follows)

CHILDREN
1 cup marinara sauce
½ tablespoon butter or olive oil (optional)

❝*The pesto was wonderful. I would not have tried spaghetti squash without this recipe. Something new for us.*❞

Pierce the spaghetti squash several times with a knife and microwave at full power for about 5 minutes to soften. Use a sturdy knife to cut the squash in half lengthwise, then scoop out the seeds. Place the squash, cut side up, in a microwave dish with about 1 inch of water. Cover with vented plastic wrap and microwave at full power for 15 minutes, rotating the dish after 8 minutes. Let stand, covered, until ready to serve.

Pour the marinara sauce into a microwave-safe dish, cover, and microwave at full power for 2–3 minutes.

When ready to serve, hold the squash securely in place with a kitchen towel or pot holder. Scoop out the spaghettilike strands with a fork into a large bowl. Season with salt.

For the children, place the squash on individual plates. Top with a pat of butter, if using, stirring to combine. Place the heated marinara sauce on top and garnish with Parmesan cheese.

For the grown-ups, place the squash on individual plates. Season with pepper and top with Spinach Walnut Sage Pesto. Garnish with Parmesan cheese.

SPINACH WALNUT SAGE PESTO

2 garlic cloves, peeled
5–6 ounces packaged fresh spinach
   or about 4 cups well-washed
   fresh spinach
15 fresh sage leaves
2 tablespoons walnuts

2 tablespoons balsamic vinegar
2 tablespoons fresh lemon juice
¼ teaspoon salt
1–2 tablespoons walnut oil
Salt and pepper to taste

To the bowl of a food processor, add the garlic, spinach, sage, walnuts, balsamic vinegar, lemon juice, and salt. Process at high speed until chopped, scraping down the sides of the bowl several times. Pour the walnut oil in a thin stream through the shoot with the motor running at low speed until the mixture begins to swirl around the bowl. Season with salt and pepper. Serve over spaghetti squash.

GROWN-UPS
Calories 250; Calories from fat 110
Total fat 13 g; Saturated fat 1 g
Cholesterol 0 mg; Sodium 400 mg
Carbohydrate 32 g; Dietary fiber 8 g
Sugars 3 g; Protein 7 g

CHILDREN
Calories 120; Calories from fat 25
Total fat 2.5 g; Saturated fat 1.5 g
Cholesterol 5 mg; Sodium 270 mg
Carbohydrate 21 g; Dietary fiber 5 g
Sugars 5 g; Protein 3 g

Spinach Pine Nut Basil Pesto: Substitute pine nuts for the walnuts and 6–7 basil leaves for the sage. Use extra-virgin olive oil instead of walnut oil.

ARTICHOKE AND RED PEPPER
RISOTTO & PARMESAN CHEESE
RISOTTO

Time to table: 30–35 minutes   Serves 2 adults and 2 children

Risotto is fast replacing pasta as a staple for easy midweek meals. Risotto is just as versatile, and vegetables, meat, or seafood can be added to customize the meal to the taste preferences of the family. Unlike other rice, arborio rice, the kind most often used in this country to make risotto, is cooked uncovered. The whole process takes about 25 minutes. Hot broth is added to the rice in stages, then stirred a few times until absorbed. In between stirrings, there is plenty of time to set the table and make a salad. The real secret to making a good risotto is to keep the stock at a constant simmer and cook the rice over a *medium temperature*. When the broth is added, the rice mixture should continue to bubble. If the heat is too high, the broth evaporates before it has time to be absorbed and the rice can burn. This dish goes well with Mixed Citrus Salad or Garlic Roasted Broccoli or Asparagus.

❝Risotto is new for us. Good combination of flavors. Will try with seafood, too.❞

4½ cups or more low-sodium, fat-free chicken broth
½ tablespoon olive oil or butter
2 large shallots, peeled and chopped fine, about ½ cup
2 garlic cloves, minced
1 cup arborio rice
¾ cup dry white wine
1 teaspoon grated lemon zest
2 tablespoons lemon juice
¼ cup grated Parmesan cheese

GROWN-UPS
½ tablespoon chopped fresh rosemary

1 7¼-ounce jar roasted red peppers, rinsed and drained
1 10-ounce package frozen artichoke hearts, thawed
Salt and pepper to taste
Chopped flat leaf parsley for garnish

CHILDREN
½ cup cooked peas or your children's favorite vegetable
Salt to taste
Grated Parmesan cheese for garnish

Bring the broth to a boil, reduce heat, cover, and maintain at a simmer.

Heat the olive oil in large sauté pan or skillet over medium-high heat for about 2 minutes. Add the shallots and garlic. Stir until the shallots begin to soften, about 2–3 minutes. Add the rice and stir until blended. Pour in the wine and stir until mostly absorbed, 4–5 minutes. Pour about 1 cup of stock into the rice. Stir frequently until the stock is mostly absorbed, about 5 minutes. Continue adding the stock and stirring until the rice is creamy on the outside and tender on the inside, about 25 minutes. Stir in the lemon zest, lemon juice, and Parmesan cheese.

Transfer half of the risotto to another dish. Fold in the peas, season with salt, and garnish with more Parmesan cheese.

To the remaining risotto, stir in the rosemary, roasted red peppers, and artichokes. Season with salt and pepper. Heat through and garnish with more chopped parsley, if desired.

GROWN-UPS
Calories 360; Calories from fat 45
Total fat 5 g; Saturated fat 1.5 g
Cholesterol 5 mg; Sodium 750 mg
Carbohydrate 53 g; Dietary fiber 10 g
Sugars 7 g; Protein 16 g

CHILDREN
Calories 350; Calories from fat 70
Total fat 8 g; Saturated fat 4 g
Cholesterol 15 mg; Sodium 560 mg
Carbohydrate 39 g; Dietary fiber 4 g
Sugars 5 g; Protein 19 g

Sun-Dried Tomato and Spinach Risotto: Substitute ½ cup well-drained julienned sun-dried tomatoes and one package of thawed frozen spinach for the roasted red peppers and artichokes, and feta cheese for the Parmesan.

Roasted Butternut Squash Risotto: Substitute 2 cups diced roasted butternut squash for the red peppers and artichokes. Replace the rosemary with 1 tablespoon fresh thyme.

Sweet Onion and Feta Cheese Risotto: Sauté until tender two large Vidalia, Maui, or other sweet onions, and use in place of the red peppers and artichokes. Replace the rosemary with 1 tablespoon fresh thyme. Replace the Parmesan cheese with feta cheese.

Onion and Bacon Risotto: Sauté 2 large sweet onions and 6 slices of chopped Canadian bacon and use in place of the red peppers and artichokes. Omit the rosemary.

Seafood Risotto: Substitute ½ pound cooked shrimp, crab, or lobster for the red peppers and artichokes. Substitute 2 tablespoons chopped fresh basil or Italian parsley for the rosemary.

LINGUINE WITH CLAM SAUCE
& LINGUINE WITH LEMON
BUTTER SAUCE

Time to table: 20–25 minutes   **Serves 2 adults and 2 or 3 children**

This deliciously light recipe for linguine with clam sauce has evolved over many years. Virtually all the fat has been eliminated, but the flavor is still rich. White wine, shallots, garlic, lemon, and parsley are combined with clams to make the tasty sauce. For the children, linguine is tossed with butter, a little lemon juice, and Parmesan cheese. Try putting some of the clam sauce in small bowls so that the children can have a taste. This entrée goes well with Italian Herbed Broiled Tomatoes, Garlic Roasted Broccoli, or Mixed Citrus Salad.

❝The children loved the pasta and tried some of the sauce. We enjoyed the clam sauce—healthy, too.❞

8–10 ounces dried linguine
Freshly grated Parmesan cheese for
    garnish
Chopped flat-leaf parsley for
    garnish

1 8-ounce can whole baby clams
2 tablespoons dry white wine
1½ tablespoons cornstarch
2–3 tablespoons fresh lemon juice
¼ cup chopped flat-leaf parsley

GROWN-UPS
2 medium-size shallots, minced
    fine, about ½ cup
4 garlic cloves, minced
1 8-ounce bottle clam juice

CHILDREN
½ tablespoon butter
1 tablespoon fresh lemon juice
¼ cup grated Parmesan cheese

Bring 2 quarts of water to a boil. Cook the linguine according to the package instructions. Drain, pour back into the pot, and cover to keep warm until ready to serve.

Heat a nonstick skillet over medium-high heat for 2 minutes. Add the shallots and garlic. Stir until soft, 2–3 minutes. Add the clam juice and drain the juice from the clams into the skillet; bring to a boil and cook for 2–3 minutes. Whisk together the white wine and cornstarch. Slowly pour the mixture into the skillet, while stirring. When the sauce has thickened, in 1–2 minutes, add the clams, lemon juice, and parsley. Heat through and cover to keep warm until ready to serve.

Toss the linguine for the children with butter, lemon juice, and Parmesan cheese. Serve the linguine on individual plates. Top the linguine for the grown-ups with the clam sauce. Garnish with Parmesan cheese and parsley.

GROWN-UPS
Calories 480; Calories from fat 24
Total fat 3 g; Saturated fat 0.5 g
Cholesterol 55 mg; Sodium 590 mg
Carbohydrate 78 g; Dietary fiber 5 g
Sugars 8 g; Protein 32 g

CHILDREN
Calories 310; Calories from fat 70
Total fat 8 g; Saturated fat 4.5 g
Cholesterol 20 mg; Sodium 230 mg
Carbohydrate 46 g; Dietary fiber 4 g
Sugars 3 g; Protein 13 g

ASIAN NOODLES WITH ROASTED RED
PEPPERS & NOODLES WITH PEAS

Time to table: 20–25 minutes   Serves 2 adults and 2 or 3 children

Here angel hair pasta is seasoned with an Asian-inspired sauce. The pasta and peas are cooked together in the same pot to save cleanup time. For the grown-ups, the pasta is then mixed with roasted red peppers, cilantro, and green onions. The spicy Asian-style sauce completes the dish. For the children, pasta and peas are accented with a milder variation of the sauce. This pasta goes well with Citrus Jicama Slaw, Orange Ginger Glazed Snowpeas, and Mixed Citrus Salad.

8–10 ounces angel hair pasta
1½ cups or a 10-ounce package
    frozen peas or other family
    favorite vegetable like broccoli,
    snowpeas, or asparagus
Sesame Ginger Sauce
    (recipe follows)

Toasted sesame seeds for garnish

GROWN-UPS
1 7¼-ounce jar roasted red
    peppers, chopped
2 green onions, sliced thin
½ cup chopped fresh cilantro

*"Liked cooking the peas with the pasta.
The sauce was terrific."*

Bring 2 quarts of water to a boil. Cook the noodles according to the package directions. Two minutes before the noodles are ready, add the peas. Bring back to a boil and cook until the noodles are done. Drain, pour back into the pot, and cover to keep warm until ready to serve.

When ready to serve, transfer the children's servings to another dish. Toss with the children's version of the Sesame Ginger Sauce and garnish with sesame seeds.

To the remaining pasta, add the roasted red peppers, green onions, and cilantro. Pour the Sesame Ginger Sauce over the pasta and mix well. Garnish with toasted sesame seeds.

SESAME GINGER SAUCE

⅓ cup rice vinegar
2 tablespoons low-sodium soy
    sauce
1 garlic clove, minced
1 green onion, chopped fine
1 teaspoon grated fresh ginger
    or ½ teaspoon dried

2 teaspoons dark sesame oil
2 tablespoons fresh lime or lemon
    juice

GROWN-UPS
½–1 teaspoon red chili sauce

Whisk together the rice vinegar, soy sauce, garlic, onion, ginger, sesame oil, and lime juice, omitting any ingredients that the children dislike. Transfer about half of the sauce to another dish and set aside for the children. Add any ingredients that were omitted and the red chili sauce to the adult variation.

Italian Noodles: Toss with spaghetti sauce and and garnish with Parmesan cheese.

GROWN-UPS
Calories 330; Calories from fat 40
Total fat 4 g; Saturated fat 0.5 g
Cholesterol 0 mg; Sodium 700 mg
Carbohydrate 61 g; Dietary fiber 8 g
Sugars 9 g; Protein 13 g

CHILDREN
Calories 300; Calories from fat 30
Total fat 3.5 g; Saturated fat 0.5 g
Cholesterol 0 mg; Sodium 320 mg
Carbohydrate 55 g; Dietary fiber 8 g
Sugars 5 g; Protein 11 g

THAI NOODLES WITH SPICY PEANUT

SAUCE & NOODLES WITH

PEANUT SAUCE

Time to table: 20–25 minutes   Serves 2 adults and 2 children

T his Thai-inspired noodle dish incorporates peanut butter, one of my children's favorite foods, into the sauce. For the grown-ups, a spicy peanut sauce with garlic and ginger seasons strands of angel hair pasta. Fresh basil and mint leaves add a delightful burst of flavor. For the children, a more mildly flavored peanut sauce is used. This dish goes well with Mixed Citrus Salad, Orange Curry Carrot Slaw, and Garlic Roasted Asparagus.

> ❝Great sauce, just like in one of my
> favorite restaurants.❞

8–10 ounces angel hair pasta or
  Asian-style noodles
1 pound snap peas or snowpeas, or
  other family favorite, rinsed and
  trimmed
Peanut Sauce (recipe follows)
1–2 tablespoons chopped dry-
  roasted peanuts for garnish

GROWN-UPS
4–5 fresh mint leaves, cut in thin
  ribbons
4–5 fresh basil leaves, cut in thin
  ribbons
2 green onions, chopped fine

Bring 2 quarts of water to a boil. Cook the pasta according to the package directions. Two minutes before the pasta is done, add the snap peas. Bring back to a boil and cook for 2 minutes. Drain, pour back into the pot, and cover to keep warm until ready to serve.

Serve the pasta for the children on individual plates with the mild Peanut Sauce spooned over the top. Garnish with chopped peanuts, if desired.

Toss the pasta for the grown-ups with the mint, basil, and green onions. Serve on individual plates and spoon the spicy Peanut Sauce over the top. Garnish with chopped peanuts.

PEANUT SAUCE

2 tablespoons peanut butter,
  smooth or chunky
¼ cup rice vinegar
¼ cup low-sodium, fat-free chicken
  broth
1 teaspoon grated fresh ginger

2 garlic cloves, minced
2 tablespoons light soy sauce
2 teaspoons honey

GROWN-UPS
½–1 teaspoon red chili sauce or ½
  teaspoon red chili flakes

Whisk together the peanut butter, rice vinegar, broth, ginger, garlic, soy sauce, and honey. Transfer half of the sauce to another dish and set aside for the children. To the remaining sauce, stir in the red chili sauce.

GROWN-UPS
Calories 370; Calories from fat 90
Total fat 10 g; Saturated fat 2 g
Cholesterol 0 mg; Sodium 520 mg
Carbohydrate 57 g; Dietary fiber 10 g
Sugars 11 g; Protein 17 g

CHILDREN
Calories 370; Calories from fat 90
Total fat 10 g; Saturated fat 2 g
Cholesterol 0 mg; Sodium 520 mg
Carbohydrate 57 g; Dietary fiber 10 g
Sugars 11 g; Protein 17 g

THE GRAND FINALE

Desserts

SUMMER BERRIES WITH AMARETTO CREAM & SUMMER BERRIES WITH WHIPPED CREAM

Time to table: about 15 minutes   Serves 2 adults and 2 children

In this wonderful summer dessert, mixed berries are sweetened with just a touch of sugar and topped with a rich-tasting Amaretto Cream. For my children, who haven't yet developed a discerning palate, pressurized whipped cream straight from the can is always a special treat.

"Nice and easy. Liked the Amaretto Cream. Almonds added a nice touch."

4 cups mixed berries, rinsed and drained
2 tablespoons granulated sugar
2 tablespoons toasted sliced almonds

GROWN-UPS
Amaretto Cream (recipe follows)

CHILDREN
1/4 cup light whipped cream

Chill four long-stemmed dessert dishes or wide-mouth champagne glasses. If the children are quite young, use plastic bowls instead of the glass dessert dishes.

Gently mix the sugar and berries together and allow to stand for about 5–10 minutes. Divide the berries evenly among the dishes. Drizzle the Amaretto Cream over the berries for the grown-ups. Garnish with a light sprinkle of almonds. Top the remaining berries with light whipped cream for the children. Garnish with almonds, if desired.

AMARETTO CREAM

1 ounce light cream cheese
2 tablespoons powdered sugar

1 tablespoon Amaretto

With a spoon, mix together the cream cheese, powdered sugar, and Amaretto.

GROWN-UPS
Calories 200; Calories from fat 45
Total fat 5 g; Saturated fat 2 g
Cholesterol 10 mg; Sodium 60 mg
Carbohydrate 34 g; Dietary fiber 8 g
Sugars 28 g; Protein 3 g

CHILDREN
Calories 150; Calories from fat 60
Total fat 7 g; Saturated fat 3 g
Cholesterol 15 mg; Sodium 5 mg
Carbohydrate 24 g; Dietary fiber 8 g
Sugars 18 g; Protein 2 g

Strawberries With Grand Marnier Cream: Substitute sliced strawberries for the mixed berries and Grand Marnier for the Amaretto.

STRAWBERRIES WITH GRAND MARNIER & STRAWBERRIES WITH VANILLA

Time to table: 15 minutes   **Serves 2 adults and 2 children**

F resh strawberries are accented with Grand Marnier for the grown-ups and vanilla for the children. This easy dessert is a wonderful way to end a nice summer meal.

❝*Never tried Grand Marnier with strawberries before. We love the combination of flavors. So simple yet so delicious.*❞

2 pints fresh strawberries, rinsed,
    stemmed, and sliced
2 tablespoons granulated sugar
Fresh mint sprigs for garnish

GROWN-UPS
2 tablespoons Grand Marnier

CHILDREN
1 teaspoon vanilla extract

Chill four long-stemmed dessert dishes or wide-mouth champagne glasses. If the children are quite young, use plastic bowls instead of the glass dessert dishes.

Gently mix the strawberries and sugar in a mixing bowl. Transfer half to another bowl. Add the Grand Marnier to one of the bowls, stirring gently to combine. Add the vanilla extract to the other bowl, stirring gently to combine. Let stand for 10 minutes.

Spoon the strawberries with Grand Marnier into two dessert dishes for the grown-ups. Spoon the strawberries with vanilla into the remaining dessert dishes. Garnish with mint.

GROWN-UPS
Calories 90; Calories from fat 5
Total fat 0.5 g; Saturated fat 0 g
Cholesterol 0 mg; Sodium 0 mg
Carbohydrate 20 g; Dietary fiber 3 g
Sugars 16 g; Protein 1 g

CHILDREN
Calories 70; Calories from fat 5
Total fat 0.5 g; Saturated fat 0 g
Cholesterol 0 mg; Sodium 0 mg
Carbohydrate 16 g; Dietary fiber 3 g
Sugars 13 g; Protein 1 g

MIXED MELON WITH RUBY RED PORT
& MIXED MELON CUP

Time to table: 20 minutes   Serves 2 adults and 2 children

Light and fruity flavored, ruby red port highlights the flavor of fresh melon in this dessert. For the children, maple syrup adds a touch of sweetness.

❝We eat a lot of fresh melon in the summer. This sweet dessert was easy to make. The port really brought out the flavor of the mixed melon.❞

4 cups diced mixed melon like
   honeydew, cantaloupe,
   Crenshaw, or casaba
Fresh mint sprigs for garnish

GROWN-UPS
¼ cup ruby red port

CHILDREN
2 tablespoons maple syrup or
   honey

Have ready four dessert dishes. Divide the melon evenly among the dishes. Pour the port over melon for the grown-ups. Pour the maple syrup over the melon for the children. Let stand for a few minutes. Garnish with mint.

GROWN-UPS
Calories 110; Calories from fat 0
Total fat 0 g; Saturated fat 0 g
Cholesterol 0 mg; Sodium 15 mg
Carbohydrate 22 g; Dietary fiber 1 g
Sugars 20 g; Protein 1 g

CHILDREN
Calories 110; Calories from fat 0
Total fat 0 g; Saturated fat 0 g
Cholesterol 0 mg; Sodium 15 mg
Carbohydrate 29 g; Dietary fiber 1 g
Sugars 27 g; Protein 1 g

CHERRIES JUBILEE SUNDAES & WARM CHERRY SUNDAES

Time to table: 30 minutes   **Serves 2 adults and 2 children**

This classic dessert sauce is usually served over ice cream. Here the cherries are poached with vanilla and cinnamon, then the sauce is thickened. While kirsch or brandy are more traditional additions to the sauce, I've substituted Cherry Marnier, a cherry-flavored liqueur.

1 cup cherry or apple juice
1 tablespoon lemon juice
1 cinnamon stick
½ vanilla bean, split in half
2 cups pitted fresh bing cherries or
   frozen cherries
1 tablespoon cornstarch

1 tablespoon water
2 cups nonfat or low-fat vanilla ice
   cream or yogurt

GROWN-UPS
1–2 tablespoons Cherry Marnier
   or other cherry-flavored liqueur

Combine the cherry juice, lemon juice, cinnamon, and vanilla bean in a medium-size saucepan. Bring to a boil, reduce heat, cover, and simmer for about 10 minutes. Add the cherries and simmer until tender, about 5 minutes. Remove the cinnamon stick. Scrape the seeds from the vanilla bean into the sauce and discard the pod. Mix the cornstarch with the water and pour into the cherries. Stir until thickened, about 1 minute.

Scoop 1/2 cup of ice cream into four individual dessert bowls. Spoon half of the sauce over the ice cream for the children. Serve at once.

Stir in the Cherry Marnier to the remaining sauce. Spoon the sauce over the ice cream for the grown-ups. Serve at once.

GROWN-UPS
Calories 250; Calories from fat 10
Total fat 1 g; Saturated fat 0 g
Cholesterol 0 mg; Sodium 85 mg
Carbohydrate 48 g; Dietary fiber 2 g
Sugars 38 g; Protein 7 g

CHILDREN
Calories 200; Calories from fat 10
Total fat 1 g; Saturated fat 0 g
Cholesterol 0 mg; Sodium 85 mg
Carbohydrate 42 g; Dietary fiber 2 g
Sugars 32 g; Protein 7 g

BURGUNDY POACHED CHERRIES &

SPICED POACHED CHERRIES

Time to table: 25 minutes to prepare and several hours to chill
Serves 2 adults and 2 or 3 children

Here cherries are poached in white grape juice and spices. The cherries are then removed from the liquid. The liquid is reduced to concentrate the flavors. For the grown-ups, burgundy adds a more sophisticated flavor. The cherries poach very quickly, but to infuse the fruit with full flavor, allow to chill for 6–8 hours.

❝Really wonderful. I liked the combination
of spices, kind of peppery and sweet.❞

1 cinnamon stick
2 cardamom pods, split, or 4
    whole cloves
4 black peppercorns
3 teaspoons freshly grated orange
    zest
2 teaspoons freshly grated lemon
    zest

2 cups white grape or apple juice
¼ cup sugar
2 teaspoons balsamic vinegar
1 pound pitted fresh cherries

GROWN-UPS
1 cup burgundy

Tie the cinnamon stick, cardamom, peppercorns, orange zest, and lemon zest in cheesecloth to form a bundle. Add grape juice, sugar, balsamic vinegar, and the spice bundle to a 2-quart saucepan. Bring to a boil, reduce heat, cover, and simmer for 10 minutes. Add the cherries and bring back to a boil. Reduce heat and simmer for 2 minutes.

Using a large slotted spoon, transfer the cherries to two separate bowls. Bring the poaching liquid back to a boil and allow to reduce to about 1 cup, 5–10 minutes. Pour 3/4 cup of the liquid over the cherries for the children.

Pour the burgundy into the saucepan with the remaining liquid and the spice bundle. Bring back to a boil and allow to reduce to 3/4 cup, about 10 minutes. Pour the mixture over the cherries for the grown-ups.

Cool the cherries to room temperature. Cover and refrigerate for 6–8 hours to allow the flavors to blend.

GROWN-UPS
Calories 290; Calories from fat 10
Total fat 1 g; Saturated fat 0 g
Cholesterol 0 mg; Sodium 20 mg
Carbohydrate 51 g; Dietary fiber 3 g
Sugars 47 g; Protein 2 g

CHILDREN
Calories 210; Calories from fat 10
Total fat 1 g; Saturated fat 0 g
Cholesterol 0 mg; Sodium 10 mg
Carbohydrate 49 g; Dietary fiber 3 g
Sugars 46 g; Protein 2 g

Burgundy Spiced Pears: Substitute cranberry juice for the grape juice and peeled, cored, and halved pears for the cherries.

MADEIRA POACHED PEACHES &

CINNAMON POACHED PEACHES

Time to table: 20 minutes to prepare, several hours to chill

Serves 2 adults and 2 children

The Madeira gives this dessert a sophisticated adult flavor. Apricots, nectarines, pears, and plums are all delicious prepared this way as well. The fruit poaches quickly, in a matter of minutes, but to infuse the fruit with flavor, allow to chill for 8–10 hours.

2 cups apple juice
1/4 cup sugar
2 teaspoons balsamic vinegar
2 teaspoons orange zest
1 cinnamon stick

1/2 vanilla bean, split in half
4 medium-size firm-ripe peaches,
    about 1 pound

GROWN-UPS
1/2 cup Madeira

Add the apple juice, sugar, balsamic vinegar, orange zest, cinnamon, and vanilla bean to a 2-quart saucepan. Bring to a boil, reduce heat, cover, and simmer for 10 minutes.

Peel the peaches and cut into 1/2-inch slices. Add the peaches to the poaching liquid. Bring to a boil, reduce heat, cover, and simmer for 3 minutes. Using a large slotted spoon, transfer the peaches to two separate bowls. Bring the liquid to a boil and reduce by half. Scrape the seeds from the vanilla bean into the liquid and discard the pod. Pour half of the poaching liquid over the peaches for the children. Add the Madeira to the remaining poaching liquid. Bring back to a boil and allow to reduce by half, about 10 minutes. Pour the liquid over the peaches for the grown-ups. Break the cinnamon stick into two pieces, adding a piece to each of the bowls. Cool to room temperature. Cover and refrigerate for 8–10 hours.

GROWN-UPS
Calories 270; Calories from fat 0
Total fat 0 g; Saturated fat 0 g
Cholesterol 0 mg; Sodium 10 mg
Carbohydrate 53 g; Dietary fiber 4 g
Sugars 49 g; Protein 1 g

CHILDREN
Calories 180; Calories from fat 0
Total fat 0 g; Saturated fat 0 g
Cholesterol 0 mg; Sodium 0 mg
Carbohydrate 46 g; Dietary fiber 4 g
Sugars 42 g; Protein 1 g

CHAMBORD BERRY SHORTCAKE &
···

MIXED BERRY SHORTCAKE
··

Time to table: 10 minutes to prepare and 15–20 minutes to chill
Serves 2 adults and 2 children

F resh summer blueberries and raspberries are steeped in Chambord, a raspberry-flavored liqueur. Use a ready-made pound cake or angel food cake to assemble this dessert in no time.

❝*Very delicious and easy to make.*❞

1 cup fresh blueberries, rinsed and
  drained
1 cup fresh raspberries, rinsed and
  drained
4 slices fat-free or light pound cake
1 cup nonfat whipped topping

GROWN-UPS
2 tablespoons Chambord or other
  raspberry-flavored liqueur
1–2 tablespoons sugar or to taste

CHILDREN
2 tablespoons cherry or apple juice
1–2 tablespoons sugar or to taste

Divide the berries between two mixing bowls. Gently stir the Chambord and sugar into the berries for the grown-ups.

Gently stir the juice and sugar into the berries for the children. Let stand for 15–20 minutes.

Assemble the shortcake by arranging slices of pound cake on individual dessert plates. Divide the Chambord berries between two plates for the grown-ups. Divide the remaining berries between the plates for the children. Garnish with whipped topping.

GROWN-UPS
Calories 190; Calories from fat 40
Total fat 4.5 g; Saturated fat 0 g
Cholesterol 0 mg; Sodium 220 mg
Carbohydrate 32 g; Dietary fiber 3 g
Sugars 23 g; Protein 2 g

CHILDREN
Calories 190; Calories from fat 40
Total fat 4.5 g; Saturated fat 0 g
Cholesterol 0 mg; Sodium 220 mg
Carbohydrate 36 g; Dietary fiber 4 g
Sugars 27 g; Protein 2 g

KAHLÚA TIRAMISU &

CHOCOLATE TIRAMISU

Time to table: 25 minutes to assemble and several hours to chill

Serves 4 adults and 4 children

Tiramisu is a classic Italian dessert made with ladyfingers moistened with espresso and Marsala, then layered with mascarpone (an ultrarich cream cheese) and chocolate. Here the mascarpone cheese is replaced with light cream cheese and whipped topping, cutting the fat calories considerably. For the grown-ups, the cake is moistened with a mixture of espresso and Kahlúa. For the kids, the cake is sweetened with chocolate syrup. Allow at least two hours to chill before serving. This dessert can be made up to several days ahead.

> ❝This was to die for. I loved it. Rich tasting and delicious.❞

1 fat-free pound cake, cut into 16
slices
6 ounces light cream cheese, at
room temperature
⅓ cup packed light brown sugar
½ teaspoon ground cinnamon
Half of an 8-ounce container of
fat-free frozen whipped topping,
thawed
Cocoa powder for dusting

GROWN-UPS
½ cup espresso or strong coffee
(instant coffee is fine)
2 tablespoons Kahlúa

CHILDREN
2 tablespoons chocolate syrup
½ cup warm water

Have ready eight 4½-ounce ramekins or custard cups. Place a slice of cake into each of the ramekins, squeezing it to fit. Mix the espresso and Kahlúa together. Sprinkle half of the mixture over four of the ramekins for the grown-ups. Mix the chocolate syrup with the water. Sprinkle half of the mixture over the four remaining ramekins for the children.

Place the cream cheese, brown sugar, and cinnamon in a mixing bowl. Mix with an electric mixer at low speed until well blended. Increase speed to highest setting and whip for about 30 seconds. Scrape the cream cheese from the beaters. Fold in the whipped topping. Spoon a well-rounded tablespoon into each of the ramekins, spreading evenly with a spoon. Dust with cocoa powder. Place another slice of cake into each of the ramekins. Moisten the cake as before with coffee or chocolate syrup, taking care to keep the adults' and children's separated. Divide the remaining cream cheese among the ramekins and dust with cocoa. Cover with plastic wrap and chill for several hours before serving.

GROWN-UPS
Calories 260; Calories from fat 50
Total fat 6 g; Saturated fat 3 g
Cholesterol 15 mg; Sodium 520 mg
Carbohydrate 45 g; Dietary fiber 0 g
Sugars 37 g; Protein 6 g

CHILDREN
Calories 260; Calories from fat 50
Total fat 6 g; Saturated fat 3 g
Cholesterol 15 mg; Sodium 530 mg
Carbohydrate 46 g; Dietary fiber 1 g
Sugars 38 g; Protein 6 g

ALMOND SHERRY BASMATI RICE PUDDING & ALMOND VANILLA BASMATI RICE PUDDING

Time to table: 25 minutes to prepare and several hours to chill
Serves 4 adults and 4 children

Sweet and nutty tasting, this rice pudding is made with basmati rice. Almonds add texture but can be omitted from the children's servings. The pudding is delicious all by itself but also makes a perfect base for Cherries Jubilee Sauce or Lemon Sauce.

**❝We use a lot of basmati rice in our everyday
meals because it cooks so quickly and has such a
wonderful flavor. The vanilla and almond really
bring out the unique flavor of the rice. The
sherry added a nice touch, too.❞**

3½ cups 1 percent milk
2 teaspoons vanilla extract
1 teaspoon almond extract
⅓ cup sugar
½ teaspoon salt
1½ cups basmati rice, rinsed in
 cold water
¼ cup blanched slivered almonds

Sliced almonds for garnish

GROWN-UPS
2 tablespoons cream sherry

CHILDREN
Raisins or chocolate chips for
 garnish

Have ready eight ramekins or custard cups. Combine the milk,
vanilla extract, almond extract, sugar, salt, and rice in a medium-size
saucepan. Cook, uncovered, over medium-high heat, stirring occasionally, until the mixture begins to bubble, about 10 minutes. Reduce
heat, cover, and simmer for 15 minutes. Remove the cover and stir
until the milk is fully absorbed. Stir in the almonds.

Spoon half of the pudding into four ramekins. Stir the sherry into
the remaining pudding. Spoon into the remaining ramekins. Garnish
the pudding for the children with raisins, forming a smiling face, if
desired. Garnish the pudding for the grown-ups with sliced almonds.

Cool to room temperature, then cover with plastic wrap and chill
several hours. If desired, unmold the pudding onto dessert plates and
serve with Cherries Jubilee Sauce, page 190, or Lemon Sauce, page
199.

GROWN-UPS
Calories 330; Calories from fat 45
Total fat 5 g; Saturated fat 1.5 g
Cholesterol 5 mg; Sodium 270 mg
Carbohydrate 60 g; Dietary fiber 0 g
Sugars 18 g; Protein 10 g

CHILDREN
Calories 320; Calories from fat 45
Total fat 5 g; Saturated fat 1.5 g
Cholesterol 5 mg; Sodium 270 mg
Carbohydrate 60 g; Dietary fiber 0 g
Sugars 18 g; Protein 10 g

BREAD PUDDING WITH APPLE
BRANDY SAUCE & BREAD PUDDING
WITH LEMON SAUCE

Time to table: about 1 hour   Serves 3 or 4 adults and 3 or 4 children

A simple and delicious baked dessert, bread pudding is made with cubes of bread saturated in a sweet and spiced custard mixture. The pudding can be served warm or cold and can be made several days ahead and reheated in the microwave just before serving.

Vegetable cooking spray
2 large eggs
2 egg whites
1 12-ounce can evaporated skim
    milk
¼ cup pure maple syrup
½ teaspoon cinnamon
2 teaspoons vanilla extract
¼ cup raisins
¼ cup chopped dried apples

4 cups well-packed day-old Italian
    or French bread, cut into
    ½-inch cubes
Boiling water

GROWN-UPS
Apple Brandy Sauce (recipe
    follows)

CHILDREN
Lemon Sauce (recipe follows)

Set oven temperature to 325 degrees F. Coat a 9 × 12-inch shallow baking dish with cooking spray and set aside.

In a large mixing bowl, whisk together the eggs, egg whites, milk, maple syrup, cinnamon, and vanilla. Add the bread, stirring until fully saturated. Fold in the raisins and dried apples. Pour into the prepared baking dish. Place the baking dish in a roasting pan. Add enough boiling water to come halfway up the sides of the baking dish. Place in the oven and bake until the custard is set in the center, 40–50 minutes.

For the grown-ups, serve the warm bread pudding with Apple Brandy Sauce. For the children, serve the warm bread pudding topped with Lemon Sauce or a scoop of vanilla ice cream.

APPLE BRANDY SAUCE

1½ cups apple juice
2 tablespoons raisins
¼ cup finely chopped dried apple

2 tablespoons brandy
1 tablespoon butter

Combine the apple juice, raisins, apple, and brandy in a medium-size saucepan. Bring to a simmer over low heat. Cover and simmer for 20 minutes. Uncover and simmer until reduced to about 1 cup. Add the butter and stir until melted. Serve warm.

LEMON SAUCE

3 tablespoons lemonade
   concentrate, thawed
1 tablespoon sugar
¼ cup water

¼ cup 1 percent milk
¼ teaspoon grated lemon zest
2 teaspoons cornstarch
1 tablespoon butter

Whisk together the lemonade, sugar, water, milk, lemon zest, and cornstarch. While stirring, bring the mixture to a boil over medium-high heat. Cook for 1 minute. Add the butter and stir until melted. Serve warm.

GROWN-UPS
Calories 350; Calories from fat 50
Total fat 6 g; Saturated fat 2.5 g
Cholesterol 65 mg; Sodium 320 mg
Carbohydrate 62 g; Dietary fiber 4 g
Sugars 39 g; Protein 10 g

CHILDREN
Calories 300; Calories from fat 50
Total fat 6 g; Saturated fat 2.5 g
Cholesterol 65 mg; Sodium 330 mg
Carbohydrate 53 g; Dietary fiber 2 g
Sugars 30 g; Protein 10 g

STRAWBERRY GRAND MARNIER

MOUSSE & STRAWBERRY MOUSSE

Time to table: 20 minutes to prepare, several hours to chill
Serves 4 adults and 4 children

This mousse is deliciously light with a hint of orange and vanilla. The grown-ups' variation is further flavored with Grand Marnier. Substitute raspberries, blueberries, or cherries for the strawberries, if desired.

Easy to make and delicious, too. Our two children loved it with more whipped cream on top.

1 envelope unflavored gelatin
⅓ cup orange juice
1 pint fresh strawberries, washed and hulled
½ teaspoon freshly grated orange zest
¼ cup honey

1 teaspoon vanilla
2 cups light nondairy whipped topping
Strawberries for garnish
Orange zest for garnish

GROWN-UPS
2 tablespoons Grand Marnier

Have ready eight 6-ounce dessert cups. Sprinkle the gelatin over the orange juice and allow to soften for a few minutes. Heat the gelatin in the microwave for 1 minute at full power. Stir to dissolve and set aside to cool.

Using a food processor, process the strawberries until well chopped. Add the orange zest, honey, and vanilla. Process until well blended, scraping down the sides of the food processor bowl as necessary. Add the gelatin mixture and process for several seconds until mixed through. Pour into a large mixing bowl.

Gently fold in the whipped topping. Pour half of the mixture into four individual dessert cups and garnish with strawberries. Stir 2 tablespoons of Grand Marnier into the remaining mixture. Pour into the remaining dessert cups and garnish with orange zest. Chill for several hours until set.

You may substitute one 8-ounce container of sliced frozen strawberries for fresh strawberries. Omit the honey.

GROWN-UPS
Calories 170; Calories from fat 50
Total fat 6 g; Saturated fat 0 g
Cholesterol 0 mg; Sodium 0 mg
Carbohydrate 26 g; Dietary fiber 2 g
Sugars 18 g; Protein 2 g

CHILDREN
Calories 150; Calories from fat 50
Total fat 6 g; Saturated fat 0 g
Cholesterol 0 mg; Sodium 0 mg
Carbohydrate 24 g; Dietary fiber 2 g
Sugars 16 g; Protein 2 g

AMARETTO APRICOT AND PEAR CRISP & APRICOT AND PEAR CRISP

Time to table: 1 hour   Serves 6 to 8 adults and 6 children

Dried apricots and fresh pears are combined in this deliciously sweet dessert. Amaretto accentuates the fruity flavor of the adults' variation while vanilla and almond extracts intensify the apricot flavor of the children's variation. Cardamom and cinnamon add an exotic twist. The crumbly topping gets its crunchiness from rolled oats, wheat germ, and chopped almonds.

Vegetable cooking spray
6 ounces Mediterranean-style dried
  apricots
5–6 firm-ripe Bartlett pears, about
  2 pounds
1½ tablespoons fresh lemon juice
¼ cup honey
2 tablespoons cornstarch
¼ teaspoon ground cardamom or
  ground cloves
½ teaspoon ground cinnamon

GROWN-UPS
1 tablespoon Amaretto

CHILDREN
  ¼ teaspoon vanilla extract
  ¼ teaspoon almond extract

2 tablespoons chopped almonds
⅓ cup brown sugar
⅓ cup wheat germ
⅓ cup rolled oats
⅛ teaspoon ground cardamom or
  ground cloves
¼ teaspoon ground cinnamon
1½ tablespoons unsalted butter,
  melted

"*Great winter dessert. My kids loved it with vanilla ice cream.*"

Preheat oven to 350 degrees F. Coat the insides of eight 6-ounce custard cups with cooking spray.

Coarsely chop the apricots and place in a large mixing bowl. Peel, core, and chop the pears into 1-inch pieces and add to the mixing bowl. Squeeze the lemon juice over the pears as they are chopped to prevent discoloration. Add the honey, cornstarch, cardamom, and cinnamon. Stir gently to combine. Transfer half to another dish. Stir in the Amaretto and pack evenly into four of the prepared custard cups. Stir the vanilla and almond extracts into the remaining mixture and pack into the remaining four custard cups.

In a small mixing bowl, combine the almonds, brown sugar, wheat germ, oats, cardamom, and cinnamon. Slowly drizzle the butter into the mixture while stirring with a fork until the butter is evenly distributed. Spread the topping evenly over the custard cups. Place on a baking sheet and bake for 35–40 minutes. Serve warm or at room temperature.

GROWN-UPS
Calories 220; Calories from fat 40
Total fat 4.5 g; Saturated fat 1.5 g
Cholesterol 5 mg; Sodium 0 mg
Carbohydrate 45 g; Dietary fiber 5 g
Sugars 29 g; Protein 4 g

CHILDREN
Calories 220; Calories from fat 40
Total fat 4.5 g; Saturated fat 1.5 g
Cholesterol 5 mg; Sodium 0 mg
Carbohydrate 45 g; Dietary fiber 5 g
Sugars 29 g; Protein 4 g

Peach and Apple Crisp: Substitute peaches and apples for the apricots and pears.

Cranberry Apple Crisp: Substitute cranberries and apples for the apricots and pears. Replace the almonds with walnuts or pecans.

CHOCOLATE KAHLÚA CHEESECAKES
& CHOCOLATE CHEESECAKES

Time to table: 40 minutes Plus 1–2 hours to chill
Serves 4 adults and 4 children

Chocolate and Kahlúa make the perfect match in this rich-tasting cheesecake. Topped with a fresh raspberry sauce, the dessert looks decadent. For the kids, the Kahlúa is replaced by more chocolate.

❝Great cheesecake. The flavors were rich.❞

Vegetable cooking spray
1 8-ounce package Neufchâtel or
   light cream cheese
1½ cups nonfat ricotta cheese
1 egg
1 cup granulated sugar
½ cup cocoa
¼ cup all-purpose flour
1 teaspoon vanilla extract
¼ teaspoon salt

3 tablespoons fat-free chocolate
   syrup
2 tablespoons semisweet mini
   chocolate chips
Raspberry Sauce (recipe follows)

GROWN-UPS
2 tablespoons Kahlúa

CHILDREN
Mini chocolate chips for garnish

Preheat oven to 325 degrees F. Coat eight ramekins with cooking spray.

Add the cream cheese, ricotta cheese, and egg to a food processor and process until well blended. Add the sugar, cocoa, flour, vanilla, salt, and chocolate syrup. Process until smooth, scraping the sides of the bowl as necessary. Transfer the mixture to a mixing bowl. Fold in the chocolate chips. Spoon half of the mixture into four of the prepared ramekins. Fold the Kahlúa into the remaining mixture and spoon into the remaining ramekins.

Place the ramekins on a baking sheet and bake on the middle rack of the oven for 30 minutes, until set. Remove from the oven and cool to room temperature. Cover with plastic wrap, refrigerate, and chill before serving. Serve with Raspberry Sauce.

RASPBERRY SAUCE

2 cups raspberries, fresh or frozen   *2–3 tablespoons powdered sugar*
1 teaspoon fresh lemon juice

Purée the raspberries in the food processor. Work the purée through a fine wire mesh strainer with a spatula or wooden spoon. Stir in the lemon juice and powdered sugar until blended.

GROWN-UPS
Calories 280; Calories from fat 60
Total fat 7 g; Saturated fat 4 g
Cholesterol 45mg; Sodium 290 mg
Carbohydrate 45 g; Dietary fiber 4 g
Sugars 37 g; Protein 11 g

CHILDREN
Calories 270; Calories from fat 60
Total fat 7 g; Saturated fat 4 g
Cholesterol 45 mg; Sodium 290 mg
Carbohydrate 43 g; Dietary fiber 4 g
Sugars 35 g; Protein 11 g

INDEX